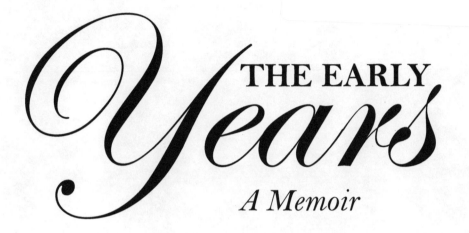

THE EARLY Years

A Memoir

Rachel G. Carrington

BOOKSIDE Press

BookSide Press
877-741-8091
www.booksidepress.com
orders@booksidepress.com

"….it is Carrington's entertaining, romantic, and well-written story of her unexpected discovery of the man who will become her life partner that makes this book the most enjoyable."

-Excerpt from the US Review of Books

"…. a story of faith and devotion to family…. Whether readers desire acknowledge of history or inspiration for everyday life, they will be sure to enjoy (this book)."

-Excerpt from a professional review by Pacific Books

"A beautiful coming of age autobiography of a woman from a small town in Kentucky. This incredible lady withstood all the challenges life threw at her. It was amazing to read how she happily faced those challenges to be with the love of her life despite all the odds stacked against her. I find the fact that she succeeded in marrying him, and was able to lead a successful life, to be an inspiration to all people. It gives hope to those who hold on to their dreams that despite all the challenges in life, if they persevere, they will succeed in their goal. A remarkable story of trust between two people that stood the test of time and how they managed to be in touch with each other despite the enormous hardships they faced in their individual lives."

-Excerpt from a professional review by International Review of Books

Dedication

This book is dedicated to my husband, Bradley, for without him my life would have been a totally different story.

Bradley E Carrington
November 20, 1920 to December 31, 2009
A Hui Hou Kakou, E Ku'u Aloha1.*

*Translation from the language of Old Hawaii: Until we meet again, my love.

Acknowledgements

First, to my sister Dee; without her, my book would not have been possible. My chance to meet my soul mate would have come and gone without her urging me to give him a chance.

Second, to my sister Alli, who was an infant when I left my childhood home. She encouraged me to tell my story so that she and the sisters who came after her could get to know me. And after hearing it, she urged me to put it in writing for all to read.

These aforementioned sisters are no longer with us, as they have been called Home. A hui hou kakou, Ke Aloha kaikainas. Aloha No Au Ia 'Oe!*

Just as important as the foregoing—to Lucy, my youngest sister, who lovingly lent me her editing skills, a lot of time listening to me reading the manuscript, and the encouragement to stick to the task.

To my sister Brandi, who was born after I left home, who avidly listened to me reading the manuscript, and who must have wiped gallons of tears while she listened.

To my daughter, Margene, who scanned my manuscript with an objective eye, looked for completed thoughts and subject continuity, and brutally pointed out what was lacking—all with a heart full of love.

And last of all but by no means least, to my friend Connie, who has a plethora of written accounts of her own outstanding, meaningful life experiences. Her memoirs, most of them written in her own beautiful handwriting, have continually urged me to write my book, as a legacy to my family if for no other reason.

God bless you all for your contributions!

*Translation: Until we meet again, beloved sisters. I love you!

Contents

Preface

The writing of this autobiography has been tardy in its coming, and the process is something I have found I needed to make my life complete. I have always kept journals, beginning in my teenage years and on throughout my adulthood. Over the years, from these handwritten records, I have written many short stories which were presented to my family and friends on their special occasions such as anniversaries, birthdays, etc. Because of the contents of these writings, these family members, my beloved husband first and foremost, and many loyal friends encouraged me to write a book, and once I started, these people greatly encouraged me throughout the writing of my life story. For this, I am eternally grateful.

Those journals no longer exist, as a major flood in 1989 destroyed most of them, and what was left I delegated to the trash heap. But one's memory is a remarkable and treasured attribute. Once I started my life story, rivers of memory began to flow.

I have lost loved ones whose deaths have left a gigantic void in my heart. The writing of this manuscript has been so very therapeutic to me by flooding my mind with fond memories of their lives, not the sad ones of their deaths.

Introduction

The writing of this book has served as the beautiful gift wrap for a very special gift God has given me. That gift is *my life*, one so fulfilled that, on looking back, I can see very little that I would ever want to change! Each hardship I experienced, each hurdle I encountered, each heartache that befell me, and each doubt I had along the way, I now see as building blocks that shaped my existence into the life I have had and the memories I have attempted to portray in this book—so very special.

1

The Formative Years

Throughout my growing-up years, we had strict rules to follow. We were a large family, becoming larger with each year, it seemed. Actually, my siblings—ten of them—and I, in most cases, were eighteen months apart in age. When school was in summer break, we all were required to do our part in the day-to-day chores assigned to us, and we accepted our routine as just normal, with no resentment. However, I learned very young that if you rapidly finished your assigned chores, you were only assigned more! I, being the firstborn in our family, had the bigger list already. At first, when given a job, I would do it as rapidly as I could for the purpose of first pleasing my mother and secondly having time for myself to play or read. I learned quickly that the result would be to have additional tasks assigned. I then realized I would have to slow down, or I would come to the point of not being able to finish at all. Some days our workload was lighter, and at those times, when we were free from our duties, we could play with the neighborhood children. I found it more difficult to find time to enjoy my favorite pastime, however. That was—and still is—reading … when I'm not writing.

Reading became a substitute for travel for me, a dream I never expected to come true, when I could find books about places far removed from my little corner of Kentucky. After I discovered what opportunities awaited me at my school library—and later at the city library—I began to have even wider choices of reading materials. From some of the periodicals on travel that I borrowed, with their enticing descriptions of places in our country, I learned that colorful travel brochures could be requested by mail from the chambers of commerce in nearby cities to the many sites grabbing my attention. The western United States and the national parks throughout the area became of prime interest to me. My desires were dreams that I did not expect to have fulfilled.

When I had read all the books, magazines, or newspapers that were available at home, I would read the print on the cereal boxes, the instructions on the new coffeepot Papa had purchased, or even the tags on the mattresses and wonder why we couldn't remove them). For some reason, my mother didn't want me to read a book … her admonishment to me was to "get your nose out of that book and find something more active to do." Later in school, the only books she found agreeable for me to read were textbooks or books that were required for book reports. I am reluctant to admit this, but in order to steal time for reading books from a library, if my mother objected when she discovered me reading, I would tell her it was required for a book report. This she would accept. It seemed that the type of book or the contents had little to do with her objections; she didn't want her children to become, in her words, bookworms, as she felt this would cause us to be lazy. At this time of my life, the ruling affected just me, as my sisters, the two next younger than me, did not like to read, and the younger ones were not yet in school.

My mother more strictly enforced her ruling when it came to reading magazines. I know now that it was the romance magazines, she wanted me to avoid, and I do more readily understand that, but I questioned some of my parents' rules for us if I could not understand the reasons behind them. I didn't verbalize those questions though, because the answer was always, "Because I said so." I didn't always obey those rules. Most rules, however, we all accepted obediently. It seemed that all others in the family at that time were more obedient than I; they just obeyed unquestionably—that is, until our brothers, the first boys born to Papa and Mama after five girls, came along. My oldest brother tended to be surly and uncooperative and often was allowed to get by with his disobedience. My younger brother had a sunny disposition and because of his cuteness was many times allowed to ignore rules and chores and do what he wanted.

My parents' rules for us, in most cases, were based on sound reasoning; they were meant to shape our character and help us become good citizens. I believe some rules concerning our clothing or the makeup we wore were handed down from both parents' religious families—but mostly from my father's family. All in all, I feel our parents did well in helping us to establish proper values for our adult lives.

Neither of our parents had an education beyond the eighth grade, and because of that, fewer employment choices had been available to them. They believed their children needed, at least, high-school educations. Thus, a good education was a priority that our parents set for us, and even though they could afford very little beyond feeding and clothing our family, they encouraged—even demanded—that we attend school, and most of us had spotless attendance records throughout our school years. The only absences I ever had were an absence because of measles and another because of the allergic reaction I had from the sting of a honeybee, both during the second grade, with no tardiness throughout elementary and high school.

Because of Papa's stressed income level, the probability was that none of us could ever expect to go beyond high school. He urged us to do the best we could while we had the luxury of attending the school he could afford. To do that, we had to be in school every day possible in the window of opportunity open to us. Today, I am grateful for my parents' efforts in putting education high on the priority list of their children's growing-up years.

When the opportunity came for me to go on to college, it was in the form of an unexpected and very lucrative scholarship offer. I had a tough decision to make! In May 1947, I stood at a crucial crossroads in my life. Late in my senior year, where before none had existed, an opportunity to go on to higher education was offered to me in the form of this all-inclusive scholarship. By that time, I had resolved to forget about college and to seek employment after high school, since I did not expect it could ever be possible to attend college. Another reason affecting my decision was that I didn't want to leave my home area.

It was in the summer prior to my senior year, when I was only sixteen years old, that I met someone I felt with the utmost certainty was the one with whom I was destined to share my life. Common sense told me that someday I may regret my decision, but the slight doubt I had did not stop me from following my dream of making a life with him, and the dream took precedence over all else in the decision that faced me. The scholarship offered would provide complete financial coverage for higher education, making lack of money no longer an obstacle. It was well-known that the scholarship was one of the most sought-after scholarships available at that time, but I strongly felt that I should turn it down, for matters of the heart tend to override all else.

I felt strongly that my parents would fight me in this decision, but I felt that I couldn't let them win. I reasoned that not telling them about my offer could work if the school personnel didn't get them involved—and so far, they hadn't. They had given me forms to complete and return upon application for the scholarship, which I had done. I had been encouraged by my elementary mentor, the principal at South Denton Elementary, to apply for it. Knowing my parents would approve its award to me if it was offered, though I would never have expected its offer, and not wanting to go through the hassle of getting my father's signature, I had signed my parents' names to the application forms. Since they were not present at any of the graduation planning meetings, they didn't learn about it until I had turned it down.

I am ashamed to admit that I was becoming increasingly and silently defiant toward my parents. I know now that young teenagers often go through this stage. I rebelled, again silently, against their authority and especially because I had rules to live by that seemed overly strict compared to those of others in my graduating class. Granted, I was a year younger than the others, which could make up for some of the difference. I have always mildly rebelled if I couldn't find a valid reason for the rule; this especially was the case when I railed against decisions, they made involving my future, for I wanted to have the upper hand in those decisions, and somewhere along the way, I closed my ears to them.

I am eternally grateful for those good people (the love of my life's voice rang loud and clear among them) who got my attention and kept me on an even keel when my parents' voices failed to reach my ears!

My mother and father were married at twenty-two and twenty-six, respectively, and became parents at the ages of twenty-five and twenty-nine. I was their firstborn, and since no reliable manual for rearing each and every child is available, they had to learn their child-rearing basics with me. With their first, second, and third child, they were stricter in every way than with those who came later, easing the reins slightly with each of them. At our last family reunion, while comparing the rules—and the strict enforcement of those rules—we older ones had as children with the rules encountered by our youngest siblings, we realized how much our parents had changed. All parents must learn what works and what doesn't, those today and those of yesteryear alike, so my conclusion is that I had just ordinary parents who loved their children and did the best they could. With each successive child, they struck out the rules and ways that did not work and eased up on others as they learned. It is just that I was first ... but I survived without scars!

Looking back, there is very little I would want to change in the life I have lived. I am just an ordinary, unrenowned, commonplace person but one who has lived an extraordinary, multifaceted, exciting, love-filled life. I am now in the September of that life, and though it has had many changes, I have a myriad of reasons for facing each day with a smile. I love to see the sun rise over the mountains each morning and set over the ocean each evening (with the much-anticipated but always unexpected bonus of a green flash). I love the leisure time but crave the busy time and experience both with equal pleasure. I am alone but not lonely. The love of my husband sustains me even though he is not physically present; he is waiting for me in a better home! The love of my children, grandchildren, and great- and great-great-grandchildren and my love for them makes my heart sing with joy! And last but never least, the love of my heavenly Father is the continuous thread that binds it all together.

2

Setting Life Goals

I grew up in a small town in Kentucky, a typical town for that time, where neighbors all knew and cared about each other. Most of us were low to middle income (depending, primarily, on the size of the family). Most heads of the household were railroad workers, the railroad being the primary job source in our town. In the surrounding areas, coal mines were numerous, and a number of men from our town worked in these mines. The remaining working people were in food service, grocery stores, furniture businesses, apparel shops, auto parts stores, office jobs, and health services with a few such professional occupations as doctors, lawyers, and teachers. Our town boasted of one public high school, two public elementary schools, and a parochial elementary school. It was increasingly necessary for our young people to move away into big cities to find employment after graduation. That could be what I would face as a graduate.

Since there seemed to always be a demand for teachers, my father encouraged me to look toward that goal after graduation. I readily agreed; I think that would have been my choice even without his urging. My father openly admitted that he had selfish reasons for wanting that career for me; he thought it would keep me in my home state of Kentucky and possibly in our hometown.

When I started into the eighth grade, and continuing through my entry into high school, I had set my goal to become a language arts teacher. My principal from elementary through junior high school seemed to recognize certain potential in me. Consequently, he showed me what great college possibilities there were for students with good

7

grades, especially those who were willing to work hard. I was eager to learn. A big part of my eagerness was due to my desire to please this wonderful teacher who was so encouraging to me, a child from a large family whose parents could not afford to send me to college. However, the main reason for my eagerness was to please my family, especially my father, who was watching my progress in school and openly admiring my zeal for learning. Without realizing it, I was setting a pattern that followed me into and through many years of my adult life. That pattern was to put pleasing others before considering my own desires. It was not because I was unselfish; I had a need for others' approval.

My father had always shown interest in my education, and even when I was just beginning school in first grade, he seemed to burst with pride with what I learned each day. On every day I came home from school when Papa was not scheduled to work, he seemed to be waiting for me to show him anything new I had learned, and I was always so pleased to tell him about the new learning experiences the day had provided. The attention from Papa was something I always craved, and I learned early in life that trying to do the best I could in school would always get his attention. He provided the money for any books I had to buy but always carefully checked the contents in order to keep abreast of what I was being taught. Also, due to shortage of money to spend on what he thought to be unnecessary, he questioned any item if he could not determine the need.

One item that I recall specifically was a periodical called *Junior Scholastic.* Each student in my class was given a copy to take home for our parents to see. The sample had an application to purchase with instructions to fill in and send back to school, and the application must be accompanied by the year's subscription cost. I don't remember how much it was, but my father, who had limited funds to spend for items not absolutely necessary, told me that I would have to do without it. I was very disappointed and started pointing out articles in the sample that were so good. I'll never forget what he told me then, for it is something that I always remember when I am viewing a sample of anything for sale.

He said, "Rachel, a sample always shows everything at its best; you just can't go on that for your decisions about a product. The magazine may be okay, but it is not a textbook, and I have to buy you textbooks. There's not enough money for everything."

Today, more than half a century later, I still tend to question any samples, my opinion mirroring my father's regarding that sample of the little periodical.

My father got a note from my teacher explaining how important the *Junior Scholastic* would be to my studies and that it was intended as a supplement to our textbooks to keep us up on current events. She also told him about a fund for which he could apply to help in buying it for me. Needless to say, my father applied for the subscription and paid for it.

He remarked, "I'll pay for my own kids' supplies."

Later in high school, the promise of scholarships delighted both my parents. In those days, few were financially able to send their children to the good schools without the assistance a scholarship provided. Consequently, it was a rarity for any parent to turn down the offer of a scholarship for his or her child.

Because of my good grades and eagerness to succeed, the principal of my elementary school in the small town of Denton, Kentucky, made the decision to heavily load my subject-matter schedule in order to move me forward more rapidly—his goal being to give me the opportunity to go earlier into higher education. With this in mind, he made the recommendation to the principal at the high school that I finish school in a three-year accelerated college-prep course rather than the four-year high-school general course work. The principal gained the necessary approval to permit it, and consequently, I went from ninth grade into eleventh grade.

Totally from my experience, I make this note of warning to anyone contemplating skipping grades or otherwise accelerating the rate of moving through high school. I don't know if it is a procedure used at all in today's curriculum, but this is one I believe should especially depend on the maturity of the student involved. I believe a lot of students may not have the maturity level to be thrust into a class filled with older students at a critical time in their emotional development and that the end result often will be that the students do not feel a part of classes where classmates are not in the same age group.

I mention the foregoing for I believe it describes my case; however, I don't feel it had any effect on my learning ability or my grades. Something I should mention here is that I was always painfully shy, and it wasn't easy for me to get acquainted with people or make friends. I found it very hard to initiate a conversation—so much so that the caption under my senior yearbook picture read "Silence is Virtue" for whatever reason the author intended. One thing for sure is that it pointed out my quiet, shy personality. That changed somewhat during my lifetime, but I easily reverted back near that stage if I stayed away from interacting with other people for long periods. Because of that, I made an effort to keep something going on in my life that would expose me to people.

3

A Birthday of Awakening

The summer of 1944 is vivid in my memory, and one instance stands out more than any other. On June 6, 1944, my sisters and I had spent the morning at vacation Bible school at our church, Church of the Pines, just up the street from where we lived. As children, we had always attended this church for Sunday school, but summer Bible school was a special treat for us. We were taught a lot of biblical verses and stories geared to help us better understand the Bible. Not only that, but we had activities and crafts to hold our interest in the three- to four-hour session each day.

At about noon, we were released to go home, and on this day, because it was my birthday, I eagerly hurried home with my sisters to see what treat awaited me. Presents were never part of this anticipation, as there was no extra money for frivolous gifts; it was just not the custom in our home. Once in my life, I did have a birthday party with gifts. It was on that day, June 6, 1936, that I became six years old, and the neighborhood girls (there were no boys there) were invited to help me celebrate. They had brought gifts! That day was a very special day for me. Mama called it my first "lucky" birthday because I was six on 6/6/1936. She went on to explain that I would be an old lady when I had my *most* special lucky birthday on June 6, 1966 (6/6/1966), for *two* numbers in the year were the same as the numbers in the month and the day of my birthday. When that birthday came, I didn't feel like an old lady, and it came and left without anything remarkable happening ... at least nothing I noticed. At thirty-six years of age, birthdays don't stand out as memorable as when you are a child.

As is usual on any of our family birthdays, Mama did have a cake, a pineapple upside-down cake. She later told us that she was not pleased with the cake, for it hadn't turned out like she expected; it was the first time she had made that type of cake. She was wrong; it was delicious!

We noticed immediately that there was a birthday cake, though Mama didn't have it prominently displayed as she usually did on birthdays. In fact, she seemed very distracted and gave little indication she even realized we had returned from church. She was listening to a small radio she kept on the back porch, where she did her ironing; ironing was a hot job, and she could get a breeze there. Back then, ironing clothes was a much warmer job than it is today, for my mother used heavy flatirons that were heated on the kitchen coal-burning range, where the fire must be kept going to provide the needed heat. Inside the homes in summertime, the heat was oppressive.

Mama's attention was solely on the radio program to which she was listening, and she had a strained look on her face. My thought was, *She's going to cry.*

It was then I noticed an unusual kind of music coming from the radio, the type of music that our neighbor, who played background music for silent movies, would play if something sad was happening. Mama finally said in a very sad, strained voice, "Walter is there." As I was later to learn, that day, June 6, 1944, was the day of the invasion of Normandy during WWII. Walter is Mama's brother, one of our favorite uncles. He was a soldier in the army. I was fourteen years old that day and knew it had to be a fearful time for my mother, but I did not understand the deep fear and helplessness Mama felt in not knowing if her brother was safe.

That birthday stands out in my memory as a time of leaving childhood and taking on a more serious understanding of what was happening outside my comfortable, protective cocoon of childhood.

4

Change to Peacetime

The ending of World War II changed a lot of lives for a lot of people; it was 1945, military servicemen were coming home, and excitement was rampant!

All home radios were constantly tuned to national news stations in order to not miss the much-anticipated news that the war with Europe and/or Japan had ended, for the current news of the war indicated the conflicts could be expected to end at any time. Major celebrations of this good news were planned, and members of our high-school band were notified and encouraged to be ready when it happened. Being a member of our high-school marching band, I, along with the rest of the band members, was called in for practice on several occasions in order to be ready, as the high-school band always played a major part of any big celebration in our little town. Schools were on summer break, and some method had to be developed for needed communication from our band director to the band members. Lack of telephones in those wartime days made communication more difficult, but our director, Mr. Gentry—a revered teacher, counselor, and friend of the students—managed this task splendidly. By the grapevine he set up, we had all been notified.

My hometown, as well as the rest of our country, was able to have two major celebrations that spring and summer, for the war came to an end on both fronts.

The war's ending with Europe in May 1945 and Japan in August that same year brought a number of young men home, many of them from my high school and surrounding areas. Some of these boys had sweethearts among my classmates who were awaiting them, and their excitement ran high. I was younger, and even though I understood their excitement, I felt just a little left out. I was only fourteen when the conflict with Europe ended and barely fifteen when Japan surrendered.

5

Sweet Sixteen: Growing Up but Hanging on to Childhood

The summer of 1946 is a year that changed my life forever! The day heralding my sixteenth birthday started out just like any other day, except it was the last day of the four-day annual vacation Bible school as well. The last day always ended with a picnic of sorts with special treats and a time for bidding teachers and classmates a fond good-bye for the summer. In past years, our picnic drink was a refreshing, inexpensive, sweet fruit-flavored drink, packaged as a powder to which water is added and served over ice. This drink was familiar to most of us who often had it at home. This year, however, it was a special treat to have soda pop (my first time ever to taste this beverage, a luxury for most of us). We had a variety of small sandwiches, potato chips, and cookies. And being my birthday, I looked forward to another treat at home, because I knew my mother would have a birthday cake for me; she always did when we could afford the ingredients. During the war and a period of time afterward, we saved the number of ration stamps it would take to purchase sugar. She always seemed to manage special treats for us, even in the leaner times that we were then experiencing. It was June 6, 1946.

Since lunch had been provided for us at Bible school and Mama had already fed lunch to our little brothers and sisters at home, we went immediately to lighting the candles on my birthday cake. I don't believe we ever outgrow the pleasure of having someone make us a birthday cake and present it with lit candles. This was a day of treats for me. Little did I know more was to come!

After we had washed the lunch and dessert dishes, I decided to shampoo my hair, for with the weekend coming up, I wanted it to be nice for church. I put the water on the stove top to heat in a small pot, since we had used most of the hot water in the range reservoir for doing the lunch dishes. The reservoir, holding about five gallons of water, was built into the end of a coal-burning range. Water heated in the reservoir when there was fire in the range, and as the fire for the noon meal was fast cooling, the stove was not hot enough for newly added water to heat. So while the small pot of water was heating on the stove top, I started hot-oil treating my hair; I usually did this prior to shampooing, for my hair tended to be dry, and the treatment made it more manageable.

Just as I had applied the olive oil to my hair, I heard a commotion in the living room and went in to check it out. I saw that we had a visitor, one of our favorite uncles, Uncle Owen! He was one of the two uncles we referred to as fairy-tale (sometimes, storybook) uncles because of all the nice things he and his brother Walter, both of Mama's brothers, did for us that brought joy to our lives. Mama offered him a piece of my birthday cake.

Uncle Owen exclaimed, "That's why I am here as well as to pick up the birthday girl and her sisters and take them to a movie!"

After eating his cake, he suggested we hop into his car (it was a major treat to ride in any car ... we didn't even own one). I remember that evening having one emotion in particular that other females in my family will certainly understand. The Gaylord girls were known for their curly, unmanageable, yet pretty hair and that they would not leave the house if one hair was out of place. Since I didn't know my uncle was coming, I had just doused my hair in very warm olive oil, and as you can imagine, that is not at all an attractive styling treatment ... not until after the hair is shampooed. As my uncle had come unexpectedly, I didn't have time to shampoo my hair and get it dried. It didn't work well unless it was combed as it dried, and that would take too much time. Without that, though, it would dry into a big, frizzy cloud of hair. What was I to do? In nothing flat, the decision was made for me.

Owen grabbed up a scarf from Mama's dresser, twisted it around my head, and said, "Now you're beautiful! Let's go!"

My vanity prevented me from enjoying this birthday outing as much as I would have without the olive oil on my hair, for I was uncomfortable while at the movie, believing that everyone around me was looking at me and noticing oil oozing through my scarf. Vanity? Oh, yes.

After Owen got our tickets and made sure we all had popcorn, we sat down to enjoy the movie. I don't remember what was showing, as that did not really matter. We even enjoyed the previews. I remember one preview in particular for a silent movie; these were still being shown in the mid-1940s. I was curious about silent movies; though I had never seen one, I had learned about them from our neighbor who played piano as background for them. He had demonstrated how his music helped to provide the emotional moods in the movies. We enjoyed listening to him practice the joyful, sad, and scary chords he played to match the actions on the screen. All in all, what really made this day so special was being able to be with our wonderful uncle.

I mention only my own birthday celebrations, as those of others in my family were, understandably, less memorable to me. My birthday arrived in the summer when school was closed with more time for midday celebrations; when school was in session, little time could be set aside in the evenings. At that time, only one younger brother, born ten years after I was, had a summer birthday. Whenever they fell—summer, fall, or winter—birthdays all rated a cake and candles.

Uncle Owen stayed overnight with us and left early the next day, promising to come again in early fall. His visits were always highly anticipated.

After my uncle left, we settled into our usual summer routine. All my sisters old enough to handle even the smallest chore were expected to complete them before any of us could go out to play. My chores usually consisted primarily of housecleaning. I didn't like housecleaning, but I learned to do all the many mundane chores needed to keep a house in order. It came in good stead when I later had a house of my own to keep!

My love for housekeeping (or should I say lack of love) has changed very little, but I do appreciate cleanliness, so I get it done.

My sister Deanna (everyone called her Dee) always seemed to get to help in the kitchen where she picked up excellent cooking skills. Mama was a wonderful cook, and Dee became a great cook, even surpassing Mama's skills. Dee didn't get much practice in housecleaning while growing up, but somehow, it didn't matter. She managed as a housewife to excel at keeping a very clean house as well. School was a different matter; she didn't do well at all. She was at top of the curve in practical skills and had a lot of common sense. She could read people well, a skill that I greatly admired in my quiet, shy little sister.

6

Leisure Fun Times

Even though it took a lot of time for chores, mostly for Dee and me (the others were too young in 1943–46 to have much in the way of chores), we still had time to play, and we sometimes played with the neighborhood children, though we mostly played with our own brothers and sisters. We rarely left our yard but on occasion were allowed to go to the opposite end of our block where there were no houses but rather a wooded area that still existed in our early growing-up years. Some of my fondest playtime memories involve that area.

One of the memories that comes to mind from that time involves several neighborhood families of children, including my sisters and me. We had had a summer storm a few days before the incident in the story I am telling; consequently, several huge trees and many large branches had been blown down by the wind, creating open areas under leafy branches where we could create playhouses for our pretend families. Our neighbors, the Partridge family, had a daughter Lowella who was about my age, as well as several younger children. Their house was on Keaton Street, a street that intersected ours (we were on the corner, with the side of our house directly across from their front porch). In our playhouse games, Lowella and I, being the oldest girls, were to act as the mothers, and we had chosen our own siblings as our children. As several real families from our block were represented here, Lowella and I divided the younger children left between us, making certain all were included in our games. There were two boys about Lowella's and my age who were to be the fathers. There was some controversy between the two of us about who was whose husband; we both wanted the same boy. The boys settled it for us, and my husband became a teenage boy we both knew from our elementary school. I did not have a crush on him, but I think Lowella did. He was actually the one we both wanted; however, for me, it was only as a pretend husband. Lowella told me later she would like someday to marry him. I don't recall the other boy, the one who became Lowella's pretend husband, but I think he was the younger of the two.

I believe the selection of husbands and the jealousy it may have created caused Lowella to feel enmity toward me, for we had some unprovoked (on my part) squabbles in our new "neighborhood." Lowella seemed to pick on my pretend family, accusing them of mischief, and if my mischievous little brothers had been a part of our house playing, I might have believed it. But she was blaming my sister Dee, who was never a mischief maker; actually, she was the epitome of a peace-loving child.

Dee was the constant companion of one of Lowella's "kids," and as the kids were together all the time, she was an easy target for Lowella to blame for anything that happened. Lowella came to me to tattle about one incident for which she was blaming Dee (I can't remember the incident), and because I didn't believe her, I would not punish Dee. Later, Dee came to me crying, saying that Lowella had spanked her for something she didn't do!

Even as a child pretending to be a parent, I had learned that even pretend parents should stay out of their kids' squabbles. But this was different; my child had been spanked by another parent for something that I believed she had not done. I went to Lowella's house to confront her about the incident, and she made a remark about the Gaylord family, calling us "poor trash," causing me to lose what little restraint I had, and I punched her hard on her chin (she was a good ten inches taller than I was, so I had to stand on my toes). She was standing holding her ice delivery (a large brick bat served as pretend ice). In those days, the only form of refrigeration most homes had was ice boxes, and ice trucks visited our neighborhood daily, delivering block ice to the homes needing it. When I punched Lowella, my immediate thought was that she would crash that brick into my head, so I jumped back. However, instead of using her ice as a weapon, Lowella grabbed my hair with her free hand but held on only briefly; she then turned and ran crying into her house. Prior to that, I had been the target of many cruel jokes at Lowella's hands, but never was she to bother me again! In fact, after a few days, we were again friends, of a sort, but there was always jealous rivalry between us.

At that end of the block and across the street from our woodsy play area was our church (Church in the Pines), which we attended from a very young age to the winter of 1944/45. Then, for some unknown reason, we changed to a church farther from home and only attended vacation Bible school at Church in the Pines. The church to which we changed, a missionary Baptist church, was South Denton Baptist. This new church seemed to have a lot more kids our age, and we continued there the rest of the time I lived at home. I especially liked going to South Denton because many teenagers from my school attended there, as well as a number of cousins from a nearby housing development for families whose menfolk were maintenance workers for the local railroad lots.

7

Summertime Adventures in the Country

Starting when I was eleven years old and Dee was ten, she and I began to spend at least part of the summer with our paternal grandmother, Minnie Gaylord, and our aunt Nancy. The reason for our visit was to help Grandma and Nancy take care of the garden that had been planted by Aunt Nancy, Grandma, and Papa. The plan was to supply fresh vegetables for both families, Papa's large family, and for Grandma and Nancy. Most of the resulting produce went home with Papa. He would come out once a week and cultivate the garden, and it was our job to finish it out and help him pick any ready-to-eat produce, which he took home for Mama to cook at home and to preserve what was left for the winter.

I loved the time spent at my grandmother's home in North Denton. I loved being in the country playing in the woods, and I marveled and delighted in the wonderful stories Grandma and Aunt Nancy would tell while we sat on the porch in the evenings just before bedtime.

I loved the great home-cooked meals they made for us using the produce they raised. Chicken was often the main entrée, for, in raising their own chickens, chicken dishes prepared in numerous ways were plentiful. All the eggs we could eat were available for breakfast and other meals as well.

I loved learning about all the setting hens they always seemed to have and could hardly wait for the eggs to hatch. If the hens made nests away from the henhouse, especially in the woods as they were prone to do, they had to be found as soon as possible. If one was found before the hen started to set, the eggs were brought to the house and the nest destroyed, for, if the hen was allowed to set on the eggs away from the henhouse, the varmints would kill the diddles (all terms used by my grandmother and aunts). It seems the chicks were safe from varmints in the henhouse. At that time, I wasn't quite sure just what *varmints* were. It turned out to mean several types of animals, ones that preyed on defenseless chickens on the nest or at roosting time.

I loved how all the animals had names and the dogs could "talk" to Grandma and Nancy, and the dogs seemed to know exactly what was said to them.

I loved going to Swede Carroll's farm, just a short walk away, to get milk and butter, for they were such friendly country people. I *didn't* like going to another neighbor's, the Roses, where we went to use a phone when Grandma went into a diabetic coma and needed a doctor, as she did on two occasions during one summer while we were there. These neighbors were also sweet people, but we were afraid of their dogs, who met us with loud, threatening barking. They told me that none of them would bite, but they couldn't convince me or Dee! And besides all that, we had to go through a deep woods covering what I now know to be ten acres; it seemed like miles to me. These were not our favorite woods, as they were very dense and dark underneath the trees, and creatures we wanted to avoid were very close before we could even see them. We often saw snakes in the Roses' woods. They were usually not poisonous, but on one occasion, we saw a copperhead that jumped five or six feet, trying to bite Papa. He killed it with a garden rake.

Another larger forest was close by Grandma's, and that forest was our favorite. Because of logging activities, those woods were not so dense, and the paths were open with sunlight flooding in.

I didn't have a great fear of snakes, but Dee did, and whether or not they were poisonous mattered little to her. The creatures that frightened me (not counting dogs) were spiders. Fortunately, I outgrew that, though I still do not touch them or want them to touch me!

I loved the smell of wood smoke that was always present in and outside Grandma's house and around the grate (a common colloquialism for fireplace). During chilly mornings and fall days, we would visit on a weekend and see a pot of shuck beans (dried green beans) or soup beans (usually pintos, but navy or other cooked dried beans were referred to as *soup beans*) merrily boiling and sending out a heavenly odor (not the shuck beans; I gagged at that odor!) to hungry visitors. Beans were cooked in a cast-iron bean pot that was used by removing a "cap" (the burner area of the stove's cooking surface) and placing the pot *into* the open area, where it fit perfectly. The pot bottom was always covered with soot and had to be precleaned before putting it into the dishwater when I did dishes (my primary duty when I wasn't in the garden). The corn bread was already baked, as that wonderful smell of fresh-baked bread indicated. If the bread was done, that meant the potatoes were done too, for we always knew fried potatoes and home-canned chow-chow (a sort of relish dish that went wonderfully with soup beans) was always ready when the bread had finished baking. We would soon all be seated along the side benches at their handmade, long wooden table, gobbling up a great meal—that is, if they hadn't prepared the shuck beans, for I never learned to like them. There are only a few food dishes that I do not like, but shuck beans still remains one of them!

We rarely visited in the winter, but I remember when we did, we would roast chestnuts in the fireplace and bake potatoes on the hearth. On rare occasions, we popped corn in a woven-wire popper with a long handle that was held over the flames. Sometimes we parched (roasted) large grains of regular corn, not popcorn. Parched grains of corn were a little hard to eat but tasted wonderful.

I loved washdays at Grandma's, when clothes were carried to Lennox River to be washed. We could wade in the shallows while being cautioned to check often for leeches, all too common in the slow-moving currents in the shallows of Lennox River. They could fasten on to you without your having felt anything; therefore, we were cautioned to check often to make sure none had attached themselves to our bodies.

On occasion, one of the dreaded leeches did manage to hook on to us. Even though their teeth are sharp and jagged, it is not painful to pull them off when they have attached themselves to your body. I later learned in a biology class why you don't feel the bite but have trouble stopping the blood flow after pulling them off. Their saliva contains an enzyme that is injected into their prey through their bite, which acts as an anesthesia, making the bite painless; consequently, the host is unaware he or she has been bitten. Secondly, the enzyme contains an anticoagulant that makes the host's blood flow freely, so the leech can feed more rapidly. If not detected and removed before it releases itself, it soon becomes engorged to several times its original size, and then it drops off the host and returns to its usual habitat at the bottom of the body of fresh water. But the wound continues to bleed, and the host can lose a considerable amount of blood before discovering he or she has been bitten. Those days in the leech-infested waters of Lennox River, we were cautioned often to check for attached leeches, and we did.

So many fond memories abound from the time spent at Grandma's house in North Denton! Little, insignificant memories of sights, sounds, and even smells abound. For instance, I loved the smell of the snuff Grandma and Nancy both used (*dipped* is the common term) and marveled at how they kept from swallowing it. I wondered why they spat so often! If they liked it so much, why did they spit it out? I wanted to taste it, and after laughing at me, they said firmly, "No!"

I loved how they carved (their term was not carving but *whittlin'*) small human figures from tree branches. (Papa was a whittler too.) Grandma, Nancy, and my uncle George (during part of this time, he was away in the army) made the small figures, dressed them in clothing Nancy had made, and placed them in a small wooden house they had built, and inside the house was hand-carved furniture, which they also had constructed. The figures all had Indian names. The one small family group of carved people that seemed to be the theme of the carvings was the Kalijah family. Much later on, my own kids saw these same figures and got to hear some of the stories from Grandma and Nancy. Other figures they had made had very humanlike heads, in miniature, which they carved from apples and permitted to dry. They looked so real, like very old and wrinkled men and women. They had delightful stories to tell about all these lifelike characters.

I loved to hear them talk about Eleanor Roosevelt, calling her by her first name only. I thought Eleanor was a dear, close friend of theirs, and I asked them when she would be coming for a visit, because I wanted to see her. They told me she was too busy helping poor people to visit them, and she probably wouldn't be coming at all, they said, because "We aren't poor." I'm quite certain that Grandma and Nancy rarely had two nickels to rub together at any one time, but what they told me about not being poor was right on! They had no money, but they were indeed *rich*!

We attended a number of Gaylord family reunions at Grandma Gaylord's home, and I have memories of spending the day playing with all my numerous cousins and seeing so many aunts and uncles, a number of them coming from a considerable distance, from as far away as Cincinnati!

One of my local cousins nearest my age was Emmajean Fields. Emmy and I were very close, possibly because we were so close in age, with my birthday coming twelve days before hers, making me the senior one. I loved being the oldest when we were in our teens; that somewhat changed when we were much older. She once warned me that it wasn't best to be the oldest and that I would get the "turkey waddle" first. At that time, I had no idea what she meant. Later, when that time of our life came, it didn't matter who was first.

Emmy is gone now, more than ten years.

It seemed like the job of washing dishes always fell to Emmy and me at family gatherings. I think we were chosen because we were considered more as the "local" cousins and therefore part of the host families. I had never washed so many dishes before or since those family reunions! Many years later in my own family reunions, my sisters and my daughter Kaylene, older than some of my sisters, seemed to take on that job. Because there were several of them working at doing the dishes, their job was not as big as Emmy and I had back in the day, and it was just the two of us.

27

For Emmy and me, large, round zinc laundry tubs (we called them washtubs) were placed on the edge of the pine-planked back porch, and we stood on the ground to do the dishes. Emmy and I seemed to get as much water on us as what ran through the cracks of the porch! Grandma's chickens gathered around our feet to pick up any food scraps that dropped through the cracks with the overflowing water.

Water for washing the dishes was heated in two big iron pots hanging over an open fire. Earlier in the day, Papa had taken on the job of drawing bucket after bucket of water from Grandma's well and filling these iron pots. When the meal was over, dish washing had to begin immediately, for Grandma was adamant that she didn't intend to feed the flies. And there were a host of them!

After dinner was over and everything was put away, Emmy and I could play with all our cousins. One year, a couple of girl cousins about our age came from a branch of the family that lived in northern Kentucky, just south of Cincinnati. We had never met them, and we immediately didn't like them. The reason we took this immediate dislike to them is because they called us their "country cousins," meant to be a put-down, and they made it plain that country cousins had to rank *way* below city cousins. They seemed to look down on us and acted as if they equated *country* to *dumbness*. When referring to the city activities, they talked about games and social events and they could tell that, in many cases, we had no idea what they were talking about. I tried to point out that I didn't even live in the country; therefore, I could not be a country cousin if I lived in the city, and I told them so.

One of the sisters smirked. "You call Denton a city? It's nothing but Hicksville, and that makes you guys country hicks."

We had never met these girls before, and we, the country hicks, decided we didn't like them either. We had had enough of their put-downs, and I had an idea how to get even.

We decided to take a bunch of the little ones for a walk in the woods and asked our city cousins to take their baby (I think it was their sister) and go along. They didn't want to take her, and the baby didn't want to go, but since several little ones near her age were with us, their parents urged them to take her, and they convinced her to go by bribing her with cookies. As we walked, they fed her cookies ... a lot of cookies! I suggested they cut back on giving the baby so many, for it might make her sick. The one called BJ told me, essentially, to butt out, that as long as the baby wanted them, she would give them to her.

After just a few minutes, while we were in the woods, the baby became sick and started vomiting. While they were seeing to her, we got our get-even plan in motion. The rest of us quietly slipped away and left them, knowing that they didn't know the woods and that the many logging roads that cut through, all looking alike, would add to their confusion, and it would be harder to find their way back. We felt there was no doubt that they would find the way back, but we knew it would take them some time. We quickly took a shortcut and got back to Grandma's farm.

After we had been home a few minutes, Grandma noticed that the northern Kentucky girls were not with us, and she called Emmy and me to her and demanded to know what we had done. We confessed, and after scolding us thoroughly, she sent us—just the two of us—back into the woods to find them, apologize to them, and bring them back to the house. We did just what she ordered. Grandma was a kind woman, but one look from her was frightening!

Though hard to eat crow, we apologized to the girls when we found them, per Grandma's instructions. We found them without a lot of trouble, for they were constantly calling out, hoping someone would hear them and come to their rescue. Even after our less-than-sincere apology, they were somewhat reluctant to follow us, for they were afraid that we might be up to more tricks. However, rather than be left again, they stuck to us like leeches. We actually were only a short distance from Grandma's and knew that the girls would have been able to get home without our help, anyway, but we felt we had saved face by going after them.

I didn't see either of these cousins again for many years; I don't know if Emmy ever saw them again. It was after Emmy's death that I saw one of them under the bright lights of the Grand Ole Opry. The girls, our northern Kentucky cousins, we had later learned, were BJ and Skeeter Davis. I believe they were sisters by adoption. When BJ was killed—I think it was in an automobile accident in her early twenties, and we heard it on radio news— Aunt Nancy told me she was a cousin, one of the girls that Emmy and I had purposely gotten lost in the woods. Many years later, when I was doing group tours and was on one of my trips, I had a group at a Grand Ole Opry performance where Skeeter was in a starring role. After the show, I talked to her, and she remembered the woods incident at our family reunion, and she laughed about it. She had no animosity toward us, because she realized it was payback and felt that they had it coming.

She added with a laugh, "And isn't it ironic that BJ and I would go into country music, for we had so looked down on country folks—or anything country, for that matter—and then what do we do? Go build a career in this kind of music!"

They (especially Skeeter) had probably made a fortune in their country-music careers. I would imagine that BJ's untimely death kept hers from being as lucrative, for it is my opinion that she could have been one of the best in her chosen career.

I fondly recall these days spent on Grandma's miniscule acreage. Tastes, sounds, and smells all come back to me as I write about our summers. Many years later as I took my own family back there for visits, the smell of Grandma's green beans and her cream-style corn produced on her small farm and cooked on her wood-burning range take me back to the days spent with her and Nancy. I don't believe I have ever tasted green beans since that taste as good as hers!

My grandmother was a strong, pioneer type of woman. She was a fun-loving, cheerful person who remained that to the end of her life. This was quite amazing for a person whose life was made so difficult for her, for she must have suffered much in her diabetic-riddled years. She was bound to a wheelchair as a double amputee for a number of years before she died. Through all her suffering, she kept her positive outlook on life.

Dee's memories did not match mine regarding the time spent at Grandma's, but there were extenuating circumstances that affected her. She could not get accustomed to the water on the farm, for it upset her stomach. Because she loved the taste of fresh-from-the-garden corn so much, she overate, and it caused her stomach problems too. She always seemed to have bowel problems. Grandma and Nancy referred to her malady as the "dwindling poo hoos," and as they would say it in a singsongy manner, it was humiliating for Dee. I don't feel they meant to be cruel, but the wounded feelings of my sensitive little sister were most obvious. I had a tougher constitution than Dee; nothing hurt me. I always felt I was so tough, and I realized later that I didn't know what being tough was. Dee suffered a lot in her life, overcoming many obstacles, proving just how tough she really was until the very end when she had to give up her fight. God gained a beautiful angel when, in her late seventies, she was called home.

8

Summer's Sweet Splendor

During the summer months when we were home rather than in North Denton at Grandma's, Mama often took us over to Aunt Haley's, Papa's sister, who lived in Section Acres, the village that was a housing development for railroad yard workers, lying southeast of Denton. This village was created for families of the workers who maintained the yards and the tracks for the local railroad switching yards in Denton.

Mama and Haley were very close, and Mama liked to visit her sister-in-law and friend. We, too, were happy to be able to visit, as we so enjoyed being with our first cousins. They were such fun-loving, multitalented kids. One of our cousins, Shelton (later referred to as Shel), was a young man of many talents, one of which was music, for he had a delightfully mellow singing voice and could play a number of stringed instruments. Another of his talents involved working with battery power and, later, wiring with electricity, making all kinds of powered items. Along with his musical talent, he used his talents involving electricity to build amplifiers and other instruments to enhance their music; he later went into the occupational field as an electrician. Shel had four brothers who were equally talented in the music arts. His three sisters could sing well, but I don't believe they played instruments. It seems that the Fields boys' and girls' musical abilities were passed down to each generation to follow in most, if not in all, descendants of Will's and Haley's family.

The Fields cousins' parents weren't as strict as ours, and the kids just had more fun than we were permitted as a result of their more relaxed freedom. Because of their musical talent, young people with similar talents would gather at the Fields' home many evenings, and we (Dee and I, especially) met lots of young people our age and older—fourteen through eighteen years old. We loved their music and developed crushes on a couple of the young boys who played music with our cousins. I don't know if the guys were even aware of our crushes.

The fun was innocent. They were good kids, but Mama was afraid that their more liberal lifestyle would have undue influence on us, and as we grew further into our teens, we were permitted to see them less often. Those summers (1943–45) were actually the only times during my teen years that we spent much time with our cousins. We would see them sometimes at church, but they were not regulars there. However, we have never lost touch, and they have always been special to us. When we stopped going there, the cousins would come to our house. Later, Mama discouraged that, saying Emmy was "too feisty" and she didn't like the boys the kids hung around with.

Another pleasant memory of that summer was that I learned to ride a bicycle and, because of that, gained some extra freedom. When we were still going to Section Acres, Emmy and I would ride our bikes around the neighborhood, and I met new people. (I didn't have a bike, but the boy cousins always made certain one was available for me when we visited.) I had my first two reciprocated crushes on boys from Section Acres after learning to ride the bicycle.

Before Mama decided that we should be seeing less of our Section Acres cousins, she permitted me to stay overnight a few times with my cousin Emmy. On those nights, we rode our bicycles around the village and, in doing so, ended up with a caravan of bikes and began to separate off into couples. A young fellow, one of my cousin Shelton's friends (on whom I had developed an earlier crush), began to ride solely with me. Later, he came along with my cousins to visit us at home, and the gang of us went for a walk up to the local elementary school several blocks away. He and I spent some time sitting on the school steps while the others played on the gym sets on the playground. So exciting! And I thought, *Is this what courting is?* His name was Will Saylor. Will was around many times during the early spring of 1946, but, as had happened before with my crushes, my interest began to wane. No incident seemed to prompt this diminishing of my interest; it just happened, even though I tried desperately to hang on to the feeling. However, my feelings changed to a feeling of guilt because of the change. Silly innocent teenage crushes!

9

Crushes

One of the boys on whom I developed a crush did not have the pristine character of others for whom I felt attraction. His name was Harry Snyder, another Section Acres boy. He had joined the army by lying about his age (he was just sixteen). He didn't want to go into the military without having a girl back home who would write him letters, and he wanted me to be that girl. I was impressed with his swagger of self-confidence and his older-beyond-his-years attitude, even though I knew he did not have the respectable character of which my parents would approve. He treated me respectfully, and I promised I would write to him. I think I wrote one letter before he was back in town on furlough.

The short length of time Harry was in service before his furlough had matured him, and the changes I discovered were not all favorable ones. He seemed to have developed the certainty that he would never come back alive —at least, he portrayed that to me, and because of his morbid belief, he wanted to "really live" while he was home. It became pretty obvious that he expected to be able to take certain liberties with me, and that was not going to happen! His one misguided attempt to touch me resulted in a stinging cheek and a dressing down from me.

As I walked away, I heard him say, "There's all kinds of girls I can get. You'll be sorry."

I was never sorry. I don't know whatever happened to him, but I heard rumors through my cousins that he served his time and left the military and did not become a war casualty. They also had heard that he had gone back to where he originally lived, some distance away from Section Acres, Kentucky.

My next and only real crush after Harry and I parted ways came in August 1946. It was not a crush at all, for that involvement showed me the differences between a crush and the real thing!

10

One Train Trip; Experiencing Two Different Worlds

Sometime in mid-July 1946, Papa told us (my sisters Dee and Josie and me) that we were going on a trip to Cincinnati to visit two of his aunts and we would meet some cousins we had never seen. Papa worked for a major railroad with a large hub in Denton. One of his primary employee benefits included trip passes for family members. Papa could apply for and acquire passes to destinations anywhere the railroad lines offered passenger train service, and Cincinnati was a major stop on this railroad. It was so exciting to be able to go on a trip, but a trip with Papa, which was so rare, made it so much more special.

We arrived in the big city of Cincinnati and were completely awestruck. My sisters—Dee, who was fourteen, and Josie, who was twelve—had never been more than a few miles from home, but I, who had the advantage of doing some band trips closer to home, felt like a seasoned traveler with a degree of expertise. Oh yeah!

Contrary to what I expected, I was in for a major surprise with the big city of Cincinnati. There were such tall buildings; Papa called them skyscrapers. There were trolleys similar to passenger cars on trains, running on tracks, but with only one self-powered car and no separate locomotive. There were trolleys without tracks that had long extended arms on top that connected to electric wires overhead that would throw sparks now and then. There were horse-drawn wagons of all kinds ... some wagon operators were selling ice, some coal, and others were collecting rags, bottles, and other sundry articles. All had drivers who were calling out their wares or what they were collecting. And on the corners were young boys selling newspapers, calling out the paper they represented, the headlines, and the price of the paper (some were three cents and some a nickel). Never had we seen such sights or heard such clatter of vehicles and voices. What an exciting arrival into this big city of Cincinnati! To get to our great-aunt's apartment (a new term for me—I couldn't wait to see what an "apartment" was), I don't remember what mode of travel we used, but it seems to have been a car—a taxi, perhaps. We went into a small drugstore so Papa could make a telephone call, and that, too, was an experience!

Papa left us standing in the back of the drugstore while he went to a phone booth to make the call. A very dark man with two little girls came into the store, and my younger sisters, who had never seen Negroes (the politically correct name for African Americans used in the '30s and beyond) were staring in awe at the little girls who had tiny pigtails covering their small heads, pigtails that jiggled when they moved. Dee and Josie were pointing at their strange hairdos and giggling and whispering about their "dirty" faces, thinking they were dirty because of the color of their skin. The father of the girls was obviously offended, and Papa, who, from his position in the phone booth, saw what was happening, hurried to us, and hustled us out of the store.

His remarked something like, "Girls, you're going to get me killed! Don't ever stare or point and make fun of somebody you see. You're in a big city, and you'll see strange sights and different kinds of people. Don't do that again."

Papa's aunt Lucy (our great-aunt) lived in a flat (What was a "flat"? I thought she lived in an apartment. So many new things in the big city.). Her apartment, or flat, was in a part of Greater Cincinnati called Oakley. It was still a big city to us, but it was on a slightly different level from anything we had experienced in the downtown area. It was not unusual to see people walking on the street carrying loaves of bread—not wrapped but in an open paper bag that covered only a small portion of the loaf or carrying an open pitcher of a foamy liquid I now know as beer or ale. On Aunt Lucy's street, we saw several small stores or delis and small mom-and-pop-style bars, all selling delightful items, such as candy, ice cream, cookies, doughnuts, and of course, the foamy liquids by the pitcherful. Such great new sights and experiences! We soaked them all in with delighted excitement. I was so intrigued by the dense foam on the drink carried in pitchers that Aunt Lucy, after bringing a pitcher home, scooped it off onto a saucer, salted it liberally, and presented it to me to drink. I loved it. That was repeated several times throughout our short stay with Aunt Lucy. Papa just laughed at the way I gobbled it up, but needless to say, when Mama found out about it later, she was horrified that he had even let me taste it. I believe the salty taste was what I liked, for as an adult, the taste of beer holds no attraction for me. After a couple of days spent with Aunt Lucy, a young man driving an automobile appeared one morning and announced he had come to take us to his mom's in Corinth, Kentucky. He was the first of many cousins we were to meet in the next few days. We headed for the home of Aunt Laura, sister to Aunt Lucy. What we saw there was the opposite of what we had experienced the first couple of days of our trip. As we traveled to Corinth, we realized we were leaving the city, and what we saw were hills and green valleys dotted with cattle, some with sheep and an occasional chicken or hog farm. And it was so quiet.

Soon we arrived at our destination to see our cousins all waiting on the front porch to greet us, as they had heard the car arrive. They offered us a cool drink of fresh well water while we waited for Aunt Laura to put the finishing touches on dinner ... and what a dinner! I have always had a great appetite, and eating is one of my greatest pleasures. I was not to be disappointed here, for the spread she provided us was outstanding. For the meat, she had roast lamb (they raised their own meat, one of the cousins informed us). She had several vegetables ... green beans, corn on the cob, pickled beets, coleslaw, some of the very best corn bread—slathered with home-churned butter—that I had ever eaten, and all the milk we could drink. Dining heaven!

I was to learn that this meal was not a special feast cooked up for company but an everyday occurrence at this home. I later realized that people who live on farms always seem to have this type of meal with the fresh vegetables in season and canned or frozen vegetables when they were not in season. Meat is harvested and preserved for all seasons ... this is farm life. Growing up in a small town, we lacked this opportunity and depended greatly on what we could purchase from the occasional produce peddler coming into town.

In spite of our small-town limitations, our parents, for the most part, provided well for us. Mama was very thrifty and wisely used what she had on hand in order to provide our wholesome meals. When produce was readily available, she canned and preserved what she could get for the winter season, and of course there were almost always dried beans to cook. There were times, however, that there was very little food in our house. We were a proud family, and something we tried to hide from the neighbors—though I doubt we were even minutely successful—was that Papa had a problem. I really don't know if he was an alcoholic or a binge drinker. There were periods of time (actually less, rather than more) when he would slip "off the wagon," and even though he seemed to miss no work, many paychecks didn't make it home. In those times, it called for every skill poor Mama had in order to feed us.

Our visit to our aunt in Corinth, Kentucky, was certainly a pleasant few days for my sisters and me. Aunt Laura's children had chores to do during the morning, but they were always free by early evening. Then let the games begin! Our fun-loving cousins introduced us to games like Annie Over, a new version of hide-and-seek, and in one of the games, we learned what is meant by "being left holding the bag." Here, Snipey, Snipey! We played many other new (most of them fun) games, as well as the games we knew from home. Needless to say, we had a wonderful time. Our cousins included two boys, a nineteen-year-old (newly discharged from the military) and one fifteen-year-old boy. There were also two girls, one twenty-one (recently discharged from the US Army WAACs) and the other a mentally challenged young woman whose age I did not know. They all joined in our nightly games. I developed a crush on Eddie, the older boy, and had to constantly remind myself he was my cousin. I suspected the younger boy cousin, Art, had a crush on me. Many years later, he confirmed it for me, and we had a good laugh about it. I never admitted to my crush on Eddie though, and I never saw Eddie again after our summer visit with them. Our pleasant visit with Aunt Laura and her family came to an end, and we reluctantly headed back to the train depot and home.

11

Surprises Keep Coming

One morning, shortly after arriving home from Cincinnati, we were surprised by a visit from another fairy-tale uncle! Uncle Walter had been away in the US Army, and after having been discharged, he was on his way back to a job in Cincinnati, the one he'd left when he was drafted into the army. (Uncle Walter was the uncle mentioned earlier who was in the invasion of Normandy.) Uncle Walter worked on the Ohio River paddle wheeler the Island Queen; I believe he was a cabin steward.

In the summer months, the *Island Queen* made trips daily from Cincinnati to Coney Island and back. Uncle Walter had some time off before going back to his job, and during that time, he wanted to take my sisters Dee and Josie and me to Coney Island for a day. After he made all the arrangements necessary, he stopped at our house and told us we were to leave the next morning at four o'clock. In order to have enough time to enjoy Coney, we had to take the earliest train we could get.

Uncle Walt had made arrangements for us to stay with a friend overnight, using his small apartment. Since he was to begin work the next day, he would bunk on the *Island Queen* as he did during his twenty-eight days of work, followed by seven days of off time. His friend, a lady that Uncle Walt had introduced to us as a former girlfriend—now just a good friend—was traveling with us so that she (Janet) could bring us home on the train with her. (Walter was not returning to Denton, for his job started the next day.) Janet's parents' home was in East Denton, and, as Papa knew the girlfriend's family, he gave permission for us to make the trip with her and Walt. Otherwise, he would never have given permission for us to go without having an adult bring us home, knowing

Walt was staying in Cincinnati. Getting to ride the train twice in one summer was such a privilege. And to Cincinnati too! It was unheard of for us, who rarely ever even rode in an automobile, and we had never been to Coney Island.

Going to Coney for the day was such great excitement. Uncle Walt bought us two strips of tickets (about twenty tickets) and sat and watched us ride everything we wanted to ride while the tickets lasted. On that day, it was Crosley Day at Coney, and many of the company employees' families were there. (Crosley was a well-known manufacturing plant in Cincinnati, and among its products were radios.) As part of employee benefits, employees had been given passes to Coney with strips of ride tickets to all the activities. As some of the families were leaving before their tickets were all used, they looked for children to whom they could give them. My sisters and I ended up with many Crosley Day tickets along with those Uncle Walt bought, making enough tickets to last us all day. We took advantage of this special privilege to get our fill of rides. Uncle Walt would only stop us to make sure we ate, and then it was back to the rides.

The perfect ending of a perfect day was sitting on the back of the paddle wheeler, the *Island Queen*, on her way back down the Ohio River to Cincinnati. We sat with Uncle Walter at the stern, watching the paddle wheel turn as it pushed the steamboat through the black nighttime river, sending a white spray over the wheel and some even onto us as we headed to our home for the night. As the calliope played, we dreamed of the wonderful day we had spent at Coney Island and about how fortunate we were to have an uncle who wanted us to experience this day. He seemed to derive a special joy himself just watching us. This was a heavenly, drowsy end of a perfect day ... especially for three young girls who knew so few of life's pleasures, and for us, these rare experiences were utterly fantastic.

12

A Near Miss

Wednesday, August 14, 1946, started out like any other day with the only thing to look forward to being prayer meeting at the little Baptist church we regularly attended. Going to church was always pleasantly anticipated, because we would have the opportunity to get together with some of our friends. However, on that day, something happened that was to change my life forever!

Two of my younger sisters, ages fourteen and twelve, and my oldest brother, who had just turned six, were with me. When we arrived at church, two of my school friends, slightly younger than I, were waiting and holding seats for us. Just for background, my parents were strict about our behavior in church, and even though they were not accompanying us, we were, in most cases, very obedient to their rules ... one of which was that we were not to sit in the back of the church. The seats my friends had chosen were on the second from last row!

My girlfriends were willing, however reluctantly, to move toward the front. Another rule from our parents was to beware of the company we keep. One of their sayings when referring to that rule was "A bad apple will spoil the barrel." I always remembered and, in most cases, heeded it. Coincidently, that rule was being broken already, because the friends with whom I sat were (my mother's terminology) both "boy crazy" and "feisty." They were not really "bad apples," but they were girls with characteristics from which my mother hoped to shield us.

Churches were prime spots for boys and girls to meet, and many young people came to church specifically for that reason; the back of the church was the perfect area for that activity, hence my parents' seating preference for us was *not* that area. Another rule we would be breaking here was the one about not talking to boys.

In those days, public places were not air-conditioned, and to stay as cool as possible, windows were all open. Insects, which are attracted to light, were always flying through the open windows. That night, we were constantly swatting at large brown beetles.

Shortly after the service started, one of my girlfriends kept craning her neck to see who was sitting in the back of the church and complaining because we weren't sitting there. Suddenly, something hit and hung in my hair. Thinking it was one of the dreaded beetles coming through the open windows, I swatted at my hair just as another one hit. I asked my girlfriend to help me get it out, and she immediately told me that it was no beetle but a wad of paper thrown by a good-looking guy in the back row. In church, mind you! She was encouraging me to look back and see; she was extremely excited. Another of my parents' rules was to not turn around to look toward the back during church; we were always to keep our attention forward. So of course, I didn't turn around.

Shortly afterward, the service ended, and we prepared to leave the church. My girlfriends were in such a hurry to get outside before all the eligible guys got away that they left my siblings and me behind. When I got outside the church, my friends were talking to two young men and pointing toward me. One guy was blond, and one was a brunet. The blond was the taller one. (I later learned the two of them were good friends of long standing.)

The dark-haired guy (the more handsome one of the two) stepped forward and politely asked, "May I walk you down the street?"

I knew he directed his question at me, but I was so shy, and remembering my parents' admonition about talking to boys, I walked on past without answering.

My thoughts were running wild with excitement; he was so handsome! He had dark-brown hair and the bluest eyes. He was dressed neatly in a pair of dungarees (we now call them jeans) and a light-blue, long-sleeve, buttoned-down, open-collared shirt with sleeves folded to just below his elbows; his face and arms were smooth and tanned. On his forearm, part of a tattoo showed, and I recognized it as similar to ones I had seen on some of the returning seniors in high school who had been in the navy. And I was tongue-tied.

My two sisters were punching me and saying, excitedly, "He's talking to you. Please say yes!"

Another of our parents' rules was "No courting until you're out of high school." So I kept walking even though I so wanted to say yes. I was impressed not only by his good looks but by his soft voice and his obvious good manners. But paper wads in church?

The church was located in the middle of the block, and soon we would be turning a corner and out of sight of the handsome young man who was obviously interested in me and who had remained back at the church. My sisters persistently urged me to let him walk with me, but as much as I wanted him to, I could not bring myself to give my consent.

As we were at just the point of turning the corner and going out of his sight, Dee yelled back, "She says okay!" Then she pulled me to a stop and pleaded, "Wait until you talk to him."

When the young man caught up with us, he asked if I would like to ride in his car with him instead of walk. I explained to him that my parents were very strict, and getting into a car with him would be absolutely forbidden. He seemed to understand and suggested I wait while he took his car keys back to his buddy in order to have his car brought around to pick him up after he saw me home.

He walked me home, and while we walked, we talked. His name was Brad Carrington, and he lived in a little town not far from Denton called Sunfish. I learned that he was twenty-five years old and honorably discharged from the US Navy in April 1945 (I met him in August 1946) due to a service-connected physical condition. He had his own multifaceted business, which included a fast-food restaurant, a pool hall, and a taxi stand, all of which he had funded in part with what he called his "mustering-out pay" and some money he had saved. He told me he had stopped at the church to pick up a girl to take her to a skating rink, not a girlfriend, he explained, but just a girl who liked to skate and that he had driven her to a skating rink several times before. He told me that the girl was not at church that night, and after seeing me, he had decided to wait and meet me, if I would talk to him. And I almost didn't!

We talked about a lot of things, and I felt so good about him. However, there was one thing we did not talk about, and that single circumstance almost caused my life story to go in a very different direction.

13

Alarming Discovery

Sunday, August 18, 1946, my sisters and I arrived at the South Denton Baptist Church. I left Dee and Josie in their Sunday school class and went on to mine. Right away, I noticed a younger girl, whom I knew casually, waiting at the door to my class. When she saw me, I realized she was waiting for me. She immediately started talking to me in an angry voice as if accusing me of some personal affront to her.

"I know something about your new boyfriend that I bet you don't! Did he tell you he was married?"

My heart dropped to the bottom of my stomach! She was persistent.

"Did you know he has two and a half kids?" she asked.

Of course, I didn't know what she was talking about. She went on to say that she would be going out with him if it weren't for these complications (she couldn't possibly be a day over fourteen, about the age of my next-in-age sister, Dee). She went on to tell me that she went skating with him two or three times a week. She seemed so angry with me.

What the girl, whose name was Jessie, had told me really made me angry with the young man I had just met—that he would be so dishonest as to keep such necessary information from me, but even more so, I was disappointed in myself for being so gullible. I had planned to see him again at church that Sunday night, but I toyed with the idea of not being there to meet him. My better senses told me that he might possibly come to my home if I didn't meet him at church. I didn't want him showing up there, for I knew how my parents would react, since dating was forbidden until I finished high school, and I had yet another year to go.

51

The young man (he had told me his name was Bradley, and I had asked if I could call him Brad) was at church as he had promised. I made sure that I was surrounded by my sisters and friends so that he could not sit beside me. After church, Brad was waiting outside the building as he had the first time.

As he fell into step beside me, apparently sensing my anger, he politely asked, "Is something wrong?"

"Not if what I am hearing about you is untrue," I angrily retorted. "Is there more you need to tell me about yourself?"

He answered, "Probably the most important part of what you need to know about me. It's true; I am married, and I have two children—a boy and a girl, four and seven years old."

"And what else?" I asked.

He answered immediately, "Are you willing to hear the whole story?" At my brief nod, he continued, "My wife is six months pregnant with a third child."

Thank the Good Lord my sisters had moved on ahead to give us privacy; they knew I was upset with him, but they did not know the reason. He began the rest of what he needed to share with me in a quiet, soft-spoken manner, not making excuses but, I believe, earnestly wanting me to know exactly how things were with him.

14

True Confessions

"I came home from the navy after I was discharged and found no one home in the house I had lived in. It didn't look as if anyone had recently been there. My personal things were there, but little else. There seemed to be a few canned foods but no perishable items and very little in the way of clothing in the closet, almost as if no one lived there," he began.

I interrupted, "Didn't they know you were coming home?"

"No one knew exactly when I was coming back. I thought of that and thought maybe, since they didn't expect me, my wife might have gone to her mother's home. Since it was late, I decided to stay overnight and to go look for her and my kids the next day. My mother lived nearby, so I went to see her before starting out to locate my family. She told me that my wife had not been staying in our house, and she didn't know where she was.

"I left to try to find her and the kids. I finally found her mother and could tell right away that she seemed on the defensive and didn't intend to tell me anything. It was as plain as day that her mother, as was her nature, was dancing all around the truth. She finally told me she would get word to my wife to let her know I was home. I doubted she would, for I had known her to rarely pass on anything truthfully. She always seems to want to make trouble between us. I'm sorry, but I don't have a lot of respect for her."

Again I interrupted, "Didn't she seem to have any idea where they were?" He replied, "Nothing she would tell me, though I believe she knew. Then, two days later, after dark, Bobbie returned to our house with only one of the kids, my little boy. She told me my little girl was sick and that she didn't want to bring her out in the night air. She didn't tell me where she had left

Kaylene, but I didn't ask either.

"The next day, she told me she was leaving and that she would be back when my little girl, Kaylene, was better. Bobbie didn't say that Kaylene was at her grandmother's house; I guess I just assumed it. When she didn't come back that day, I went to Bobbie's mother's house to find Bobbie had never been there, according to Bobbie's sister, who lived close by. Her sister also told me that it had been quite a long time since she had seen Bobbie there. Again, she repeated what her mother had told me, that neither her mother nor she knew where they were. Somehow, again, I feel that neither her mother nor sister were telling me the whole story."

At this point, I interjected, "What reason would they have for not telling you? I would think they would have to know how much the children missed their dad and that they would want them to see you. How long had you been away?"

"Almost four years. My son was a baby when I left; he didn't even remember me. My little girl does, and I am sure she missed me. My mother-in-law has never liked me. She wanted her daughter to marry a doctor who was about twenty-five years older than Bobbie. I didn't have any money, and he did. For some reason, Bobbie chose me, but she was never happy with me. She'd never admit that to me, but she *never* wanted to stay home."

By this time, we had reached my home, but Brad's story wasn't finished, and I wanted to hear it all. In the meantime, I noticed that Dee and Josie had gone to the back porch steps and were sitting there quietly. Papa had gone to work, and Mama was in bed. I sure was glad that my six-year-old brother, Chandler, had not gone to church with us that night, because he was rather a spoiled child and was known to tattle and was not always truthful. When he was, it was only part truths; he tended to highly embellish any tattling on his sisters, and he was good at it. He had already gotten me in trouble by telling Mama and Papa about Brad walking me home during the past week and added a few half-truths—altogether unnecessary, for just walking with a boy would have been enough! They had really read me the riot act, pointing out the rules about not courting boys until I graduated and certainly not talking to boys in church ... actually, no talking in church, period!

I wanted badly to hear what Brad had to tell me, and I was determined to give him the time he needed. My only fear was that Mama would awaken and find us not yet in and come out to look about us. We stood in a shaded area out of sight of the only back window of the house and the back porch, and my sisters were set to warn me if someone came out of the house.

Brad reached out and held both my hands as he continued his story. "I don't know what, but it was plain that something strange was going on with Bobbie. But the next day, she came home with both kids. I was so happy to have my family home, but it didn't last. In the past, before I was drafted into service, she was prone to picking fights at the slightest provocation and using the fights as reason to leave. She would stay gone for three or four days and then return, but in a few days, she would be gone again. When she returned, no reason was ever given for her absence. That is the same thing that happened this time, and after it happened twice in the next week, with an overnight away each time, I realized it was time I was checking things out, for, by not questioning her, I was making it too easy for her to play whatever game she was playing.

"I had decided I didn't want to live like that, that it was time that I did something about it. In the meantime, I was not going to stay there and wait for her to make up her mind to stay home.

"I packed my things and moved into my parents' home. After finding that I had moved out, Bobbie started coming to my parents' home often, begging me to return to our home. I did after a few days, for I wanted to be with my kids and try to make a go of the marriage, though I had serious doubts that things would change. This time, though, she was at home for a month or so, the longest time she had ever stayed home during the entire time we had been married. At least she left only in the daytime, returning at night, and that was presumably to visit her mother. One day, one of my brothers who had been in the US Army came home, and I wanted to take the children to see him, so, thinking they were visiting Bobbie's mother, I went to get them and bring them home with me. I arrived at the home of Bobbie's mother, and no one was there. One of her neighbors told me my mother-in-law was in Ohio with one of her daughters and had been gone two weeks. In the past two weeks, my wife had left home, presumably to visit her mother, or so she had told me, on three occasions. Obviously, it had all been lies.

"I had almost given up at that point on making my marriage work. Even though my wife had stayed home recently, more than she had ever before in our marriage, she still seemed to have little to no interest in a relationship. Nothing really had changed in her efforts to try to make things between us work. We were parents now, and I felt that it was important, if only for the kids' sake, that we try. It was obvious that she didn't care."

"Why did you ever put up with this ridiculous behavior?"

"I would never have thought I would put up with anything like this, but if a marriage with kids is at stake, you will put up with a lot more, I am finding out! But now I am afraid that something is going on that I will no longer ignore. The kids may be being exposed to things they should never be allowed to be a part of, and I can't afford to let it go on. I have to get them away from the situation.

"As I told you, her actions upon my return from the navy were really nothing new; she always seemed to have a wanderlust and would come and go as she pleased. I never knew when I came home from work each day whether I would see my family or not. Early in our marriage, I put up with it, for I wanted so badly for our marriage to work; later, I stayed for the sake of the kids. Circumstances in our marriage had not changed, except that she had become really argumentative lately. She would pick arguments, putting her face in mine while screaming at me as if she was daring me to hit her! This wasn't my idea of what a marriage should be, and I was tired of living like that."

"Since you feel this way, did you ever consider divorce? If you had stayed with her and she keeps daring you to hit her, aren't you afraid you might? Are the kids around when she is screaming at you?"

"The kids are. And divorce has not been on my mind until now. I thought only of leaving her, but I didn't want to leave the kids with her.

"From the way she has been acting, I assumed she wanted me gone. When she left this time, I waited until she came home—she was away just overnight —and I told her that since it wasn't working for us I was moving back to my parents' home. She began to scream that I was not going to leave her with a couple of kids to take care of. I told her I would gladly take them with me, and she became even angrier and grabbed a broom and begin to hit me with it. She had gotten in a couple of hard blows before I could get it away from her. As I turned to walk away from her, she grabbed me in the back of my neck with her sharp fingernails. I turned and struck her with the broom, hitting her on the shoulder. She stopped fighting then and really started to cry and beg me to stay. I'd had it with her promises and I turned, gathered my things, and left for my parents' home."

"Oh my goodness!" was all I could say as he continued.

"The next few days, I spent a lot of time looking for temporary work to tide us over until I could get my business up and going and had just gotten home on the third day when the county sheriff came to my parents' home and arrested me for battering my wife with a broom.

"I had spent four days in the county jail when my mother came to bail me out. While I was there, in the idle time, I thought a lot about my situation and made up my mind that I wouldn't waste any more time in a marriage with a woman who just wouldn't settle down!

"I found a job working for a farmer who needed help to clear new ground." (This was farmland that had never been cultivated and in most cases was filled with stumps where the timber had been cut and taken away. It was prepared for planting crops by removing the stumps and the undergrowth. The undergrowth is comprised of small shrubs and a lot of briars, and it requires very hard, backbreaking labor to remove it. The process is called clearing new ground.)

"When I was at work during the day, Bobbie would come to my mother and cry about my not being satisfied with her and not wanting to make our marriage work. Apparently, she was telling my mother only about my leaving and didn't mention anything about the times she had been staying away herself. I hadn't talked to my parents about our problems, because I didn't want to worry them. They only knew I wasn't happy. But Bobbie had convinced them she wanted to make our marriage work and that the separation was only my idea. Then my mother and sisters all began to urge me to take her back, and I finally gave in under the added pressure."

"How many times have you given in like this?"

"More times than I like to admit. At least this time, she seemed more willing to stay around. It took some time for me because I had lost a lot of respect for her. Bitterness about the incident with the broom had stuck with me; while sitting idle in jail, I had had time to think. Looking back, I realized she had purposely goaded me into hitting her, and she had gotten the reaction she had wanted in order to have something to hold over me in order to have the power to get what she wanted from me.

"I moved back in but insisted on separate sleeping arrangements. The situation was awkward, but I had more hopes for the next several weeks. Then she began to come into my room each evening and cry and beg me to come back to her bed, and consequently, neither of us was getting much sleep. She finally won out, and, as she had stayed home as per her promise for several weeks, I had begun to have some hope myself that this time our marriage could work. I finally decided to do as she had been begging me to do, to give it another try—if not for me, then for the children's sake.

"Then it started again. This time, she would stay for weeks. I wanted to see my kids, so I decided I would go wherever she was to see them. One of my neighbors had told me he had seen her go into a house on Bugger Branch Road with the kids a few days before. I headed for the place where he had directed me, and when I arrived at what looked like a one-room cabin, I knocked, and Bobbie came to the door. You have probably guessed by now; she was living with a man who I found out later had probably never worked a day in his life. He didn't legally live in the cabin but was squatting there; the shack was a hunting cabin kept supplied for hunters to use for refuge from the cold while winter hunting. I figured this had been going on for a long time, starting while I was in the navy, if not before."

Incredulous, I asked, "Were the kids there?"

"They were. I saw through the open door that there was only one double bed and a baby bed, and my first question was to ask where my kids slept. She immediately told me that they slept in the baby bed. I learned later from my little girl that she slept in the same bed as her mother, at her mother's feet!

"After the proof of my suspicions that she was with another man, I decided I had no reason to stay around for a marriage to a woman who didn't love me and whose behavior had killed any feelings I had for her. I went home to talk to my folks about plans I was making to go back to Newark, New Jersey, and return to the shipyards there. Since our country was still in such turmoil in the jobs market with industrial conversion from wartime to peacetime and the business of returning military going back into their jobs, it was hard to find work.

"With no marriage to stay for and no way to provide for my family properly on one-dollar pay for a long day of backbreaking labor, I had decided that I had little choice but to go back to the job I left when I was drafted at the shipyards in New Jersey. I had written to them, and they encouraged me to come back as soon as possible, for my job was waiting for me. My buddy Nathan Hathaway, a boy who had grown up with me—he was the reason I had initially gotten the shipyards job— had heard through the plant grapevine that I was coming back. He had called his brother in Kentucky to relay to me that he had lined up an apartment for me in his building, but he wanted to make sure that it was only me coming. It seems that the building management had strict rules, and they preferred singles only, and all who lived in the building must have jobs. I called him and told him it was just me, that I had no marriage. He seemed really glad I was coming. I was still working with the farmer, and just a day's notice to him was all I needed before I left, so I left for New Jersey in just a few days."

15

One More Last Time

Brad had still more to tell me. He continued, "After Bobbie had been caught, she seemed to decide that she had too much to lose by going on as she was, so she came home. This time, she was the one to come home to an empty house. She went to my parents' home and, finding that I had left the state to return to my shipyards job, began immediately to write to me there, begging me to let her come to Newark. I would not even consider it at first, and then my mother wrote me to say that Bobbie had stored our furniture after letting our rental house go and had come to stay with my mom and dad and hadn't left for even a short time in the two weeks she had been there. My mother told me that she seemed to be very sincere in trying to make up for her mistakes, and she hoped that maybe I would consider trying once again. She also said that she would take care of the kids if I wanted to give Bobbie a try at coming to New Jersey and getting a job.

"'Since she seems to be seriously trying to make things right, a couple of weeks' trial will give you a chance to see if there is a possibility that things are ready to work for you two,' my mother pleaded."

"How could you even think of taking her back? I would think you would never even consider it!" I exclaimed.

"Because she is my kids' mother, and I believed then that it was better for a family who has children to have a mother and a father both living with them. Since then, I have decided I am wrong, for a mother and father who do not love each other and quarrel and fight in the presence of their kids aren't creating the right kind of home background. In the past, a legal separation is not something I thought I would ever consider, but now I don't see any other way.

"So, I finally caved under the pressure and told her she could come to New Jersey. I explained the apartment rules in my building, stressing that she would have to work. I also stressed that this did not mean I was taking her back but that I would see how things went and then decide what I would do. She made arrangements to come to Newark and arrived two days later, on a Thursday.

"In the two days before she arrived, I looked into possibilities for employment for her. She had no experience, for she had never been employed, and I knew that she may have a little trouble getting a job—at least one that paid well. There were a few bakeries and restaurants with hiring signs in their windows, and I got the information for them and even talked to the persons who did the hiring in a couple of them. They sounded promising. I thought one of those jobs would be a start, for I honestly didn't know how long she would last. I didn't look forward to her coming; I hadn't figured out how I would handle it.

"Since she arrived on a Thursday, she had the weekend to get used to the area and to find her way around. The jobs for which I had information were close by, and a short walk would get her to most of the jobs where I had seen the Help Wanted signs. I didn't need a car in Newark; the navy yards, where I worked, had buses for the shipyard employees to get them to work. There were area buses, but I figured if she could walk to her job, it would be less hassle for her. I took her around and showed her the area and the jobs I had checked for her. She said any of them would be all right, and she would go around on Monday to see if anyone would hire her.

"During the next week, things started happening. When I got home from work, she told me she was starting work the next day at one of the restaurants. No excitement or even anxiety showed in her actions—just a matter-of-fact statement that she was hired. The next day when I came home from work, she was sitting on the steps of our apartment building.

I questioned her about why she was off at that time of day, for most restaurants would be very busy at dinnertime.

"She said, 'I quit! The cook couldn't keep his hands off me.' "I said, 'Did you try one of the other places?'

"She replied, 'Not yet. I'll go tomorrow. You need to leave me a key. I've been sitting here for two hours.'

"I said, 'Two hours and it is just now four. That means at two, you would have had time to apply at another place, and if it was another restaurant, they may have hired you for the dinnertime rush!'

"'I don't really want to work in a restaurant!' she complained.

"'How about one of the bakeries, then?' I asked.

"'That sounds more like what I would want to do,' she replied.

"The next day, I awakened her when I left for work at six thirty. She complained about having to get up so early, but she did get up. That day when I came home, she was not there, so I assumed she had gotten the job and was working. She came home at eleven thirty that night and said that she had gotten the job and would be working second shift and didn't have to go in until two thirty the next afternoon. The next few days, she was in bed when I left for work and gone when I returned. That shift suited me fine, for I was a long way from accepting her back in my life, and she was really making no effort to act like she wanted me back. A couple of days later, the landlord stopped me when I returned from work and said he was serving notice on me and I would have to leave. The rules were clear that if a room was occupied by a couple, they both had to work; he was tired of sailors hanging around the apartments of women when their husbands were at work. I guess it was obvious to him that I had not known that was going on. He continued, saying that I had been an excellent renter until I brought my wife there and he would let me stay if I sent her packing by the next day and if he saw no other sailors there.

"I was waiting for her when she arrived at my apartment at almost midnight that night; I had noticed she was beginning to be a little later each night. I first asked her if she still had her key and then asked to see it. She looked puzzled but took it out of her pocket and held it out to me. I took it, and then I told her she was to be out of there when I left for work at six thirty the next morning, and she was not to come back into the building at all. She could stay in New Jersey or go home; I didn't care what she did, but she could not stay with me, and I would see to it that she would not be staying with my parents when she got home. I further told her that I didn't want to see her lying, sneaking face again, and I wanted her to stay out of my sight.

"It was then I learned she was pregnant. At first, I wouldn't believe her, and I sure didn't believe the baby was mine. However, I later learned that the baby's due date lined up with when she was home for several weeks and when, for a short time, she seemed to be putting forth effort to make things work.

"The rest is history. She is pregnant, and by the doctor's calculation, she will deliver sometime in late October. The baby most likely is mine, and I'll raise it. My kids are very important to me, and I intend to have them all in my custody someday. If I ever decide to marry again, my kids and I come as a package deal.

"Even with the pregnancy news—I didn't believe her at the time—I held firm to my statement that she should be out of my apartment and out of my life early the next morning. I was not so heartless as to put her out that night, but I meant it when I said she could no longer come back there. Since I had her key, she would not be able to get back in, and I felt a great sense of relief. She had not figured on this happening, for she thought I was so gullible that she could get by with it. I wonder how she figured on explaining why she wasn't getting a check when the time came? I was glad she was out of my hair during the time she was supposedly at work. I wonder how long it would have been before I suspected something if the landlord had not told me what he did. Since I was really not communicating with her, it may have taken me some time. No pay coming in from her may have clued me in, as I did expect her to pay her own way.

"By the time Bobbie returned to Kentucky three days later—I don't know or care where she spent the three days—I had been at Newark navy yards for one month. I missed my kids and missed having someone close to talk to, and I decided I didn't need to stay in Newark. I gave my two weeks' notice, and at the end of that time, I left to go back home."

I was so astounded by all this that I could say nothing!

16

Starting a New Business or Two

Brad was not yet finished, and I knew it was getting late. I didn't interrupt, however, for I wanted to hear his whole story. He continued, "While looking for a way to make a life with a little more stability for my kids, I began in earnest to try to find something I could settle into at home in order to support my family.

"My job at the shipyards had been as a welder, so I began to think about starting up a welding and repair shop as a business. I still had my mustering-out pay to purchase what I needed to open a business. And what was most important, I believed a welding shop could do well in Denton, for at that time, repair requiring welding had to be taken to a nearby city. So that is what I looked into when I got home.

"I found a suitable building, rented it on a six-month lease, and bought some used equipment from a guy going out of business. He gave me names of customers from Denton so that I could have a start and promised to send more to me. He made good on his promise, and I started out with several good customers. One of the customers was constantly trying to buy me out, offering me more than I actually had in the business.

"In a short while, I had made enough money to save a little toward a home for the future, when I would have custody of my kids. I had not changed in my resolve that they would someday live with me. As I was nearing the end of my welding repair shop's building lease, a man I knew from Rolling Rock, a town south of my parents' home in Sunfish, wanted to sell me a restaurant and pool hall. After weighing the possibilities of the business, I was in with the high rent I was paying in Denton against the very low rent for the buildings housing the existing restaurant and pool hall—which was also an established business doing fairly well—I decided to go for it. I contacted the guy wanting the welding business and told him I was ready to make the trade. Then I was suddenly in the restaurant business!

"I also had ideas of starting a taxi business, for I could see where I could make money in that area, as there was no way a person without a car could go anywhere without depending on someone else with a car to get him there. I immediately started looking for a good used car, as few if any new cars are being manufactured even yet following the war. I found just what I wanted, a '41 Plymouth with a burned-out motor. I found a completely reconditioned engine and hired it put into the $300 car for $500. The body was in perfect shape, and with the reconditioned engine, it should last several years. I was in business! That's where I am now, a year since I started this business. I have built it up, and business has been good."

I interrupted to ask, "Where do you live now?"

"I'm living at my parents', and it's working out pretty good. I don't see my kids often enough, but I do see them. Bobbie has finally decided to leave me alone, I guess. At least she seems to have accepted that the marriage is over. Since I have felt that I won't ever want to get married again, I hadn't considered getting a divorce, for divorce is unheard of in our family. Since then, I have rethought that and have come to the conclusion that if Bobbie and I have to live apart, the kids will be in the same position of only one parent in the home whether we are separated and live apart or divorced and live apart. And for a mother and father who no longer love each other and fuss and fight in the presence of their kids, we're making a bad life for them by not living apart. Most recently, I have come to the conclusion that a legal divorce is the best way. That's where I am now."

After a long pause, he continued, "I know this is a lot for you to swallow, and I don't expect you to do it all at once. I want to see you again, and if you decide you want to see me, you can let me know on Wednesday when I will be at the church, hoping to see you. If you still want to keep seeing me, tell me then. Sorry I didn't tell you all this the night we met, but as you have noticed, it took a long time to get it told, and I wanted you to know it all. My just coming up with 'I'm married and have children and a pregnant wife' the first time I saw you ... would you have ever seen me again?"

I can imagine that the look I had on my face gave him his answer.

With that, he squeezed my hand, and as he left, he said, "I'll be at church on Wednesday; please think a lot about what I have told you. Whatever you decide, I'll go along with it. Check me out in any way you want to. I have nothing to hide and have not pretended to be what I'm not. I hope you feel that you can trust me, but if you don't and don't want to see me again, I'll leave you alone."

17

An Important Decision

Even though I believed all that Brad had told me, my decision had to be made looking at the whole situation. That should have taken a bit of time, but my heart believed we could make it work, and my head couldn't sway this matter of the heart.

When Wednesday afternoon rolled around, I could barely wait for the time when I would see this man who had so quickly become very important to me. My parents were still unaware that he existed, and knowing what I then knew about him, I knew they would not accept him and would consequently prevent me from seeing him.

My sisters highly approved of Brad and wanted to see us together, and I had no fear of their tattling on me. My young brother, however, was a different story. That Wednesday night, I had to take him along, and I learned that he would accept bribes. Like any blackmail, the first payment is just the opener —especially if the perpetrator is barely six years old and has a hard time waiting until he *can* tell!

I eagerly met Brad after church and told him I believed him and that his situation did not make a difference. One fact that did not make a difference then—and never has for me—was our age difference; I was sixteen, and he was twenty-five (he would turn twenty-six in the fall of 1946).

The fact that I was a minor and he was an adult was to become a big worry for him because of the legalities involved. During all this, I did not have a clue what kind of problems and worries I was creating for my parents, let alone Brad! Brad did, and he tried to enlighten me, wanting me to understand how they felt, but I wouldn't listen, for I didn't want to hear. I was still angry with my parents. Then and throughout my life, Brad's maturity, his common sense, and his always being so levelheaded were major pluses in our lives.

18

More Hurdles

After it was obvious to my friends and others at church that we were fast becoming an item, Jessie, the girl who informed me of Brad's marriage/family status, decided it was time to make her play.

Many times, on the nights that church was scheduled, when Brad finished a taxi run (by then, he had his taxi service up and running and stayed busy operating it while he had a manager for his restaurant and pool hall), he would stop at a small café down the street from the church. Here, he would sit in their parking lot and update his daily log while waiting to see me. Jessie knew this when she saw him there, for she had mentioned it to me several times that he was waiting for me. When she saw me leaving the church, realizing Brad had not yet seen me, she would jump into his car and throw her arms around him, knowing that I would misunderstand when I arrived on the scene. Sometimes, while he waited for me, he might go into the café to get a sandwich. He would be there for only a short while, but Jessie, knowing he was waiting for me, would jump into the passenger seat, hoping I would think she was with him, and it did make me doubt him. Even though Brad had made me no commitments, it would have hurt me to see him with another girl.

Also, during the same time frame, Jessie started coming to me at church, telling me about her many dates with him. When I approached him about her actions, he was absolutely astounded.

"I made it very clear to her from the beginning that I felt she was too young for me to be with and that I was merely giving her a ride to the roller rink. I have not even taken her there in several weeks." I believed him, and I didn't let her antics bother me after that. Her efforts to come between us were fruitless, and she eventually stopped trying, or so I thought.

Brad was an expert roller skater. He and one of his brothers won many first-place prizes for their performances in skate dancing contests and other activities in roller-skating. I was never anything but mediocre. I could understand why he wanted to take Jessie roller-skating, for she made a perfect skating partner for him. He had mentioned on a number of occasions, "She's such a good sport," and I knew he admired her. At that time, Denton had no roller rink, and skaters from Denton went to Frankfurt, a town a short distance from Denton. Because I was not supposed to be dating, I couldn't find the right excuse to get away very often for the length of time it would take to go to Frankfurt. Brad had stopped transporting her to the roller rink, according to him.

Jessie was very jealous of me, and I think because of that, she may have been responsible for our next big hurdle. So far, I had never met or heard from Brad's estranged wife, Bobbie. However, she appeared one day on my mother's doorstep, very pregnant, claiming that I was hanging around her husband and was breaking up their marriage. She came while I was at school. Naturally, my parents were so shocked and so upset that I was a part of this horrendous action that I was totally grounded from all but classes at school, and no more could I participate in extracurricular activities. In other words, there would be no opportunity for me to see Brad, for my parents no longer allowed me to go to church! I believed that Jessie had somehow gotten the word to Bobbie that I was seeing Brad. Another acquaintance of mine, one of Jessie's friends, had told her mother (the mother was a friend of my mother) about Brad's connection with me, and she had warned my mother that I was going to get into trouble "fooling around with a married man." Both incidents I had connected with coming from Jessie.

19

Daniel

In May 1946, one of Brad's younger brothers was discharged from the army. Daniel was four years younger than Brad and a handsome young man—but not with Brad's darker good looks, I hasten to add, and he was not the classy dresser his brother was. Daniel was blond with blue eyes and a little taller than Brad. He had a way with the girls too. The night I met him in early September, the young ladies were flocking after him!

Fall was often the time for carnivals to come to Denton, and this year was typical, as a very popular carnival was in town, and miracles do happen—my parents allowed my sisters and me to go! I knew Brad would be there, because his restaurant was hosting a concession stand at the carnival. He was hoping that I, too, would be there, and he was prepared to have someone take his duties at the stand so he could be with me. He was accompanied by his brother when he met with me and my sisters.

This was only the second time I had seen Daniel, the first being earlier in the previous month. In the short time, his hair had grown out, and he didn't look quite as spiffy as he had earlier. I mentioned it to Brad later, and he said Daniel had been working with their dad, who was the chief brick firer at the brick plant (Denton Brick), and the heat had roughened his skin. Actually, the heat had blistered it, and it was now healing. He also hadn't had time for a haircut. Being a firer of brick means working in the open doorway of a firing furnace where bricks are finished, and the temperature is extremely high. Brad's dad's skin and neck area looked like coarse brown leather due to many years of working at this job. I guess that accounted for the difference in Daniel's appearance.

Daniel still seemed to be as popular with the girls, however. My sister Dee also was attracted and spent the rest of the evening walking hand in hand with him, a fact that seemed to worry Brad. I thought it was great! My sister with the brother of my beloved—how cool was that? Brad told me later that he felt that Daniel was too old for Dee and that he was used to running with girls much older, and it worried him because Dee was obviously very attracted to him. I later found that he had talked to his brother and had asked him to leave her alone.

20

Dee's Secret

After Brad's talk with Daniel asking him to leave Dee alone, Dee didn't mention Daniel that whole fall and winter. Granted, my sister and I weren't communicating like we once did—my fault, mostly, for I had so many secrets I had to keep from everyone. I found myself talking and sharing more with my eleven-year-old sister, Sharon, than anyone, except maybe my aunt Bettie, and I didn't get to see her very much, as she worked away from home. My sister Shar seemed to understand and support me more than the older ones, and apparently, she never told a soul the secrets we shared. Concerning Dee's relationship with Daniel, I found out much later (in June 1947) through a note from Dee (I was no longer at home) that she had a secret she wanted to share with me: she was meeting Daniel at a new roller rink that had opened in downtown Denton. It seemed that my parents had loosened the reins on the girls and that Dee and Josie were permitted to go out occasionally. In that note, she told me she was crazy about Daniel.

On July 3, 1947, I saw Daniel for the first time since the carnival in September 1946, and I asked him about Dee. He said he wasn't seeing her any longer, that he realized she was too young for him. I was puzzled. Why was their age difference, which was six years, thought to be too much, and yet the age difference between Brad and me was more than nine years, and that seemed to be okay? I posed this question to Brad, and he answered, "It isn't the years in difference in age as much as the difference in the people involved."

21

Stolen Moments

When I had been grounded from extracurricular activities (prior to this, my only other activities were honors clubs, such as Honor Society, Beta Club, Latin and Spanish clubs, and tutoring of three students), it only left the high-school football games and the time of my daily rides to school to get to see Brad. As I was a member of the high-school band, I was permitted to attend the football games, as football season had started. My parents felt that being in the band was part of my curriculum; thus, they permitted band activities. Brad came to every home game. As far as the rides to school, I couldn't get away from home any earlier than the usual time for leaving and had to be home within a reasonable time after the school day ended, so I didn't get to be with him nearly enough. However, things got better right away.

My parents were very proud of me being involved in these after-school activities, my honors clubs, and tutoring. Pulling me out of them was hurting them as much as it hurt me, I realized. After my missing one week, they relented, but not before warning me I would be watched. Granted, I was sometimes abusing the time it took to partake in these activities, for I was spending some of that time with Brad. Most of the time, he would catch me on the way and take me on to school each morning shortly after I left home and then bring me back each evening and let me off a block from home. He also took me to my club meetings and the tutoring and would bring me home afterward. (He never went to my house but left me off a block or so away.) We had time to talk almost every day, but not nearly enough time.

Tutoring was an off-and-on-again occurrence; any money received for this went to my parents for books and school supplies. Because it was an honor to be selected to tutor, I didn't want to miss any scheduled times, for only the dependable tutors would be kept on. However, in some weeks, no tutoring was scheduled, and I would still go to town as if I were tutoring (my tutoring was done at the high school) and spend the whole time with Brad. I am very surprised my parents didn't catch on to this, for I gave every penny of the money made in my tutoring jobs to them. One way Brad and I had of being together was at home football games. Being in the band gave me freedom I wouldn't have had otherwise.

At the games, all the cheerleaders and most of the band members were seeing someone and were always in couples. Brad came to every home game, and prior to the game, he watched the band march from the high school through downtown Denton to the football field (a little over a mile) as we did every home game. I was so proud he was there to watch me; there was never any family member present at the games, but I had him. Please understand that I'm not blaming my family for not being there; I never questioned their absence. But the fact is that I needed someone to be there and be proud of me. Brad made up for it one hundredfold!

Brad always stayed at the game and drove me home afterward and never failed to be there. I could spend the game break times talking to him, and that was such precious time. After football season ended, we didn't have as much opportunity to be together, but we found ways. By then, we were deeply in love. Of course, I am aware of that now; back then, I didn't know how you were supposed to know you were in love. I only felt that I had to be with him. I know now that I was head over heels in love with him. I remember asking Brad, "How can you know when you're in love?" With divorces beginning to be so prevalent, I felt you had to be absolutely sure.

22

Anticipation for Things to Come

The winter of 1946/47 was brutally cold; then and now, I never seem to be able to put on enough clothing to keep out the cold. As a child, when the katydids (insects active mostly at nightfall in late summer and believed by those living in the South to herald the coming of winter) began to sing, Mama believed that their song meant winter was six weeks away. The only depression I ever remember feeling was when the katydids began their call. This lasted throughout most of my life up until our later years when the need to work for a living was no longer there; we would leave cold Ohio—where we had chosen as our home state and where we planned to live the rest of our time together except for the winter. Then we no longer dreaded the cold weather. Depression no longer occurs when I hear the katydids; on the contrary, the sound of their chorus makes me look forward to a winter home in a warmer place where we were able to share many years together. Hawaii calls!

As children, the exciting anticipation of the Christmas holidays served to break up the monotony of the cold, damp, and dreary weather winter brought. When a child is young and still believes in the jolly, rotund elf that makes his rounds on Christmas Eve, cold-weather worries abate. The cold means the possibility of snow, and children eagerly watch for the early snowfall Santa needs for his sleigh.

Mama and Papa always made Christmas exciting for us when we were children. Even though there was little money for gifts, they somehow managed to have something for each of us under a beautiful Christmas tree, one that had magically appeared along with the gifts after we went to bed on Christmas Eve. I later learned that the tree had been brought to us by the kind souls of the little church at the end of our block. Along with the tree were small bags containing fruit, mixed candy, and nuts left over from those distributed to the children at their Christmas Eve services. This kind act was repeated in other years, and we were always extremely grateful.

Another fond childhood memory of Christmas was the opening of the large box of small items (I now think of it as "the care package") that had come from our uncles Owen and Walt, and I still can feel the exhilarating rush of eager anticipation while waiting to find out what was to be lifted next out of the box. We were never disappointed.

After the big letdown that fell upon me throughout my childhood when Christmas was over, I always looked forward to going back to school. The coming of the Easter season was almost as eagerly anticipated as Christmas. It meant that winter was almost over.

We always had a new dress for Easter. Mama was an excellent seamstress and designed and made all her daughters' clothing. Many times, she dressed us alike except for the color of the fabric. Sometimes she would let us make the color choice, and I didn't always choose the best color for me. My hair was strawberry blonde, my skin is fair, and I have blue eyes. My color choice for one beautiful dress that she planned for me was red, and the color was less than complimentary to my fair skin and reddish hair. Dee was a brunette with darker skin coloring than mine, and red looked beautiful on her. (She had chosen blue.) I tried to trade dresses with her, and she was willing, but no such luck! She was so much smaller than I that Mama said it was impossible for her to make the alterations needed for the switch of the finished dresses.

Easter meant spring was coming! With spring would come warmer weather, and we could exchange the long black or brown cotton stockings we wore for anklets (short cotton socks). Most years, Easter meant new shoes for each of us as well. On many years, Easter was not warm, and on those Easters that came early or when spring was late in coming, I recall being so very cold walking to church with bare legs in short socks, and sometimes in sandals and without a coat, for who wanted to cover a beautiful new Easter dress? We all hated the long stockings we wore in winter, but on those days, we wished we still had them on.

23

Joyful Winter Evenings

Brad's business made it harder to get away in the mornings as winter approached, and I saw him less. He had problems getting good, trusted employees to open and close his restaurant, and someone had to be there for the breakfast customers. Until he was able to find the right person to take this duty, he had to be there to open, so he came to see me only in the evenings. The long, cold walk to school was harder because I missed him so. However, it caused me to treasure even more our time together at the end of the day.

In the daytime, mostly on the weekends when I could manage to get away for a few hours, we would just go riding in his car. Most of the time, we would head south, sometimes going as far as Waltersburg, Kentucky, a little college town thirty miles from Denton. He lived at the midpoint of this drive in a small village called Sunfish, and while driving through the area, he would point out homes of his parents and local businesses along the way. We sometimes stopped at a small store and service station owned by one of his neighbors, George Stinson, and Brad would buy me an RC Cola and a MoonPie—such a treat! We never had soda pop at home; my first cola product was with him. If we had baked goods, they were home baked and not packaged products, and we had candy very rarely unless it was Christmas— when we could have several pieces as many days in a row as Santa's gift lasted—but never candy bars!

When Brad bought these treats for me, something happened then that disturbed me greatly—something we both had a laugh over later in our life together. Because such treats were a rarity for me, I savored them by eating them very slowly in order to make them last longer. Brad ate his quickly, and when he saw that a large portion of my MoonPie or candy bar still remained, he would reach over and break off a chunk and eat it. That broke my heart, for I was trying to make it last as long as I could, but he thought I was having trouble eating it all, and he was merely helping me. I had thought he was being greedy.

After a length of time that we had been together, I finally said, "Why don't you just get another if you're still hungry? I *want* mine!"

He countered with, "Oh, I thought you were having trouble eating it all, and I was just helping you finish it! Why didn't you tell me?"

Later in our life together, we would always laugh about this scenario when we remembered it.

As we drove farther south, he would show me his businesses at Rolling Rock, and sometimes we'd stop there, depending on how much time we had. When we did, he would make me a pork chop sandwich on white bread. Another treat, store-bought bread was a luxury my family could not afford. Then, time permitting, we would go farther south through an area called Gladstone, where he'd point out farms and smaller homes of relatives, all of whom I would one day meet. On rare occasions, we would venture into Greencliffe, a small town on the state border where he had more relatives— specifically, a brother James and his family. During those drives, I met none of them other than his parents, one brother, and one sister, and I later learned he felt he had no right to introduce me until he could legally claim the right to let them (and me) know his intentions. He was proud of his heritage and was proud of me, but as he pointed out, the time was not yet right.

I did get to meet his mother, and what a hardworking, frankly speaking, very knowledgeable, interesting lady! Brad had such great respect for her. It was during one of those stolen times we had found to take these long drives that I realized that there was not much he didn't share with her; she was his best friend. She knew the situation with us and apparently was aware that I was very important to her son. She feared for him, of course, but was most definitely on our side. In an aside to me, she told me that it had been a very long time since she had seen her son so happy and thanked me for my part in it.

Brad had a jukebox in his restaurant with all the current hits of the 1946 season. He also had a radio in his car, and we listened to music in those stolen moments as we took our drives. Music was important to me then, as now, and Brad, too, had developed a taste for my kind of music and for music in general. Music was just something he needed for his restaurant, for he neither liked nor disliked it. I think that he had just never had time to stop and listen. From listening to his car radio, we rapidly found a few recordings that became our favorites. On the rare occasions that I could go with him to his restaurant, we would listen to the jukebox and sing along with our favorites, but we mostly sang while listening to his car radio, for we preferred not having an audience, as neither he nor I would win any awards for our singing. What I loved most was his singing to me—as he did quite often—and I treasured those times he sang. One fun song Brad sang to me was "That's How Much I Love You" by Eddy Arnold and it went something like this:

Now, if I had a nickel,

I know what I would do.

The song goes on to talk about how the author would spend his nickel for candy and give it to his special girl to show his great love for her. It was a popular song during this time period.

Another of our favorite songs from the jukebox was an instrumental entitled "In the Mood." On his car radio, many songs of the season became favorites of ours that winter, among them, "The Old Lamplighter," Bing Crosby's rendition of "White Christmas," and another song by artists Margaret Whiting and Johnny Mercer entitled "Baby, It's Cold Outside." Such memorable times and the joy we shared those winter evenings!

24

Maturity Issues

As I was nearing my seventeenth birthday, physical maturity had been sneaking up on me. I never felt I was as attractive as the older girls in my class, for most of them never seemed to lack whatever it took to attract the boys. I thought it was partly because I did not wear makeup and they did, and I couldn't wear pants. (Jeans rolled to just below the knees was the fashion or fad of the day.) Papa absolutely forbade the wearing of any kind of makeup, and in his mind, only boys wore pants. Because it was easy to hide, I finally began to use lipstick by sneaking it to school and applying it there and diligently scrubbing my mouth clean before going home. One of our neighbors, one of the Wilmot girls, who were neighbors just across the main street from us, had given me a partial tube of lipstick, and since I had been using it daily—while not at home—for a week or two, I would soon have to have more.

Even without makeup, my newer physical maturity seemed to be attracting the wrong kind of attention. Occasionally, a young man on the street would make a pass at me, or when passing by a group of boys, I would get totally unsolicited wolf whistles. I didn't like this, and I didn't know how to handle it. I started to observe the older girls in my classes to see how they reacted, and to my surprise, they seemed flattered by this kind of attention and just flirted back. I decided not to use their method and tried to avoid placing myself in a situation where it might happen. It still happened, though less frequently.

Since I was seeing Brad less, I often walked home alone after my club meetings, for none of my club mates lived in South Denton, and no one went my direction. I didn't know when Brad would be coming into town (few had phones in those postwar days, and he had no way of contacting me). I always felt uncomfortable alone in some of the areas in which I traveled on my way home. Brad had cautioned me and had given me pointers on how to protect myself from a possible assault, though I had never had need for his instructions. I always felt that I could take care of myself, but he was quick to show me I couldn't. With just one hand, he showed me how ridiculous my assumptions were; he was able to push me to the ground and hold me there, using only his left hand (he was right-handed). I also thought I could outrun a would-be aggressor, for I had outrun all the girls in my physical education class in a recent foot race, and again, Brad proved me wrong, even though his legs were slightly shorter than mine!

This night in particular, in one of the secluded areas of the street, fronted by closed businesses with high fences and gates blocking entrance from the sidewalks, I heard a car approach from the rear. Suddenly, a harsh male voice growled, "Want a ride, sweet pea?" Startled, I glanced back to see the passenger door of a four-door sedan opened to the sidewalk, and the guy who had spoken was hanging out of the car with a leering grin on his face. Wolf whistles were coming from others in the car. On the quick glance I had taken, I saw four people in the car looking to be all males.

I was very frightened. I started to run, but with the high fence on one side and the car on the other, I had no choice but to continue on the sidewalk. The car was staying parallel to me, and two guys on the passenger side were both grabbing for me. Just as I realized I was not going to outrun them, I had started to panic, and at that very minute, a car raced up behind them with horn blaring, and the would-be assailants shot off down the street with wolf whistles trailing the car as it sped away.

My beloved Brad was in the car approaching from the rear and had, only by chance, come to my rescue! Heaven only knows what could have happened if he had not chosen to come into town that night. As it turned out, that was the last time that I had any club obligation; I was to graduate the following week on May 29. I don't think I would have had the nerve to try that nighttime walk again. The only other evening obligation I had was my graduation, and since Brad was aware my parents would not be there, he had told me that he would be there—not just to bring me home but to attend my graduation and see me receive the honors I was being awarded.

25

Plea for Change

Graduation from high school is a very special occasion in one's life, and I wanted to look my best. Mama, who usually made all my clothes, had decided to buy a ready-made dress for me, and I loved it! Store-bought clothing seemed to represent a certain status I longed to attain, and this dress would do it. It was white cotton eyelet with short sleeves, a fitted top, and gathered skirt. Earlier in the year, I had gotten a pair of white sandals with two-inch heels, and the shoes completed my ensemble. I felt very much in style and in line with what the other girls were wearing. To set off my graduation ensemble and to complete the appearance of being grown up, I needed makeup.

Through my life thus far, I had always been a favorite with Papa, and even though circumstances of late may have changed that, I knew that in order to get permission to wear a little makeup, I would have to charm him into agreeing. I had some advance preparation for what I was about to ask of him, and at that point, it was only the permission to purchase and wear lipstick. I had the money; one hurdle accomplished! I waited until he was settled and comfortable in his man cave of sorts—a corner of our living room containing his rocking chair and his radio, where he spent much of his time smoking his ever-present cigarettes, listening to the radio, and reading the newspaper or practicing his beautiful penmanship. I started with telling him I wanted to start wearing lipstick, for I would soon be seventeen years old and I thought I was old enough. I also told him that he wouldn't need to give me money for it, for I had washed dishes for a neighbor, earning sixty-five cents.

Papa began to tell me all the reasons he felt I should not wear *any* kind of makeup, and I rapidly realized my plans were not working.

I threw in my last argument. "But all the girls wear it."

Papa countered with, "And that's just the reason you won't. I don't want you to be like all the other girls!" The negotiations ended on that firm statement.

Sometime during the next week, Papa asked if he could borrow some money from me. You guessed it; he needed sixty-five cents. He made no mention of paying me back. That didn't stop me from wearing lipstick, however. Aunt Bettie, Mama's younger sister who worked in Cincinnati, was home for a visit and brought me a full tube of lipstick, and I was good to go. I had hoped she was planning to be back in town for my graduation. Since she was only a few years older than I was, I wanted someone with whom to share confidences, especially with all that was happening to me with Brad in my life. My aunt Bettie was a good listener, and she could be trusted to keep my confidences. We just didn't have time together anymore since she had her job and I had school and Brad. She knew I was still seeing him, and she had not tattled on me. Besides, she knew him to be a good man, as she had gotten to know Brad before I met him through a former boyfriend of hers who really respected him and had introduced them when Brad was in his early twenties. As far as coming to my graduation, Bettie could not attend. She had to be back on her job in Cincinnati after Memorial Day and she had scheduled a ride with a co-worker to return to her job, and they were leaving on the day of my graduation, May 29.

26

A Peek into the Future

Even though Brad and I gave the appearance of being carefree around our peers, the fear of being caught by my parents always loomed over us. The big fear was that we would be forced to be apart, and I couldn't bear that. I believed that Brad felt the same way. A fear that Brad had and did not share with me until later on was his knowledge that my being a minor would create big legal trouble if my parents wanted to pursue it. I was blithely unaware of this. Brad was still not free to make any commitment to me, for legally, he was still married.

Brad became more aware that until he was free from his marriage, it was just a matter of time before it would be impossible for us to be together. He didn't talk to me about it, but he became more cautious, spending less time with me and spending more time in public places in the company of other people. (Later, I learned that he was attempting to give the outward impression that he was no longer seeing me.) I was increasingly aware that we were spending more time apart and even had become afraid that he had grown tired of me and was moving on, though when he was with me, he was as attentive and loving as ever. During those rarer times that we were together, I felt as if his love had grown deeper, giving me mixed signals. It was something I couldn't even talk to him about. I suppose I was afraid to hear the truth. All these doubts I was feeling, and I had no one with whom I could talk about them!

Brad's new little son was born that fall, and after his birth, Brad's estranged wife made a renewed attempt to break us apart in order to get him back. She called on acquaintances to act as spies for her. Bobbie had refused to give him a divorce, and his attorney had advised him to wait until after the child was born. Of course, his attorney had also advised him to break all ties with me. Was he trying to do that?

Divorce is something that had never happened in our family, so it was an unfamiliar concept to me and carried a degree of disgrace. My religious training made me aware that, biblically, divorce is not approved, so it definitely was of concern to me. After a lot of prayer and deliberation, it still didn't matter enough to me to back out of our relationship. To have my beloved Brad in my life was so important to me that if it meant letting my life be tainted by marrying a divorced man, then so be it. I later learned that the Bible does sanction divorce where the reason is a partner's unfaithfulness. My goal, without giving it any real thought, was to get married, and my husband unquestionably would be Brad. But would we ever make it? There were so many hurdles!

I realized how unhappy Brad had been in his marriage, and I knew Bobbie wasn't happy, so I could not understand why she wanted to hang on to him. I believe it was the security he offered, as it was very clear to me that he was a hard worker and a good provider; it was obvious in the way he continued to provide for his kids and his desire to stay in their lives and to make a home for them.

Brad was concerned about the kind of life to which his kids were being exposed. He left no question in my mind about attaining his goal of getting custody of his children. He didn't file for custody along with his divorce filing; it was unheard of in those days that fathers would even be considered for custody of minor children. But he assured me he would get them, and as he had told me way back when he admitted his marital status, whoever he married had to agree to a "package deal." Recently, he had taken that statement a bit further and said to me, "Whoever I marry must love my kids!" I had not even met his kids at that time.

One warm day soon after our conversation about Brad's avid desire to gain custody of his children, we had the opportunity for one of our country drives, and as we started out, he mentioned that he wanted to make a stop. We arrived at a residence a short distance from Denton, and he stopped the car and went to a door of one of the homes. He waited on the porch a moment and then returned to the car carrying a small boy. The little boy was blond with fat little cheeks and very blue eyes. He stared at me without smiling and seemed quite shy. Brad introduced me to his son, also named Bradley.

Brad placed the little boy in the front seat between the two of us, and I noticed that, from time to time, the child glanced shyly at me. Even though I was talking to him, he didn't speak and shyly averted his eyes. However, when he thought I wasn't looking, he would glance my way as if he is wondering who I was.

We had been traveling but a few minutes when the little one started to become drowsy and would, from time to time, fall over against me. To support him, I pulled him over against my body and held him there. He aroused slightly and snuggled even closer and slept on. During all this time, Brad had not said a word, but I noticed he was closely observing his son and me. Brad had stopped at a traffic light, and I saw we had arrived in town. Because I was so engrossed in his son, I didn't even know what town. Bradley Jr. awakened and looked around, a little startled. He saw his dad and then me. He promptly climbed up into my lap and again dozed off. He was *mine* from then on. He had stolen my heart! He was four.

It was several weeks before I met Brad's seven-year-old daughter, Kaylene. She was a pretty little thing and was in the process of making mud pies under the front porch at her grandma Alene's house. (Alene Kennedy Carrington was Brad's mother.) Kaylene's dress was mussed, and she had a streak of mud on her face. She was dark blonde with eyes that were not quite as blue as her dad's. Kaylene was a bit more reserved with her affection toward me. She probably wondered what her daddy was doing with this new person. (When Kaylene was several years older, I was privy to what her thoughts were at that time and her later contacts with me. At the time of our meeting, she was older and less trusting than her little brother, so I had to earn her trust.)

It was not until after our marriage that I was privileged to meet the youngest one, Barry. At that time, he was just a few weeks over one year old.

27

Tying Up Loose Ends

The spring of 1947 brought about changes that affected Brad's and my time together. My school schedule had gotten much busier just prior to my graduation, and the many extracurricular activities—especially those of a social nature in which a high-school senior is involved—excluded those who were no longer in school. A prime example was my high-school prom. Rules concerning the senior prom forbade outsiders in attendance, so Brad could not attend. I was invited to be the date of another senior, but I had no desire to be with anyone but Brad. I turned down the young man's invitation to accompany him to the prom and gave up the opportunity of going myself. There were to be girls there without dates, and they encouraged me to join them, but to me, the prom actually seemed unimportant.

By then, I had turned down the proffered scholarship, and it was awarded to another student at another high school, a senior at Lynnville, a school district not far from Denton. (I am making an assumption here, but because of a newspaper announcement concerning the same all-inclusive scholarship award to this Lynnville High School student—which had been announced within a week after I had turned it down—my parents felt it was the same one, and I had adopted their assumption.) My senior-class advisors were appalled at me, for they said turning down such an offer simply never happened. I was afraid they would recruit my parents for further support, but fortunately for me, they did not. When my parents later learned from me that I had turned down the scholarship, they were puzzled and extremely disappointed. Except for the initial disappointment it brought my parents, though, I have never regretted my decision.

28

Pomp and Circumstance

May 29, 1947, the day of my high-school graduation, had finally arrived. Excitement was high, and the seniors were scurrying around trying to get their caps and gowns in place and to be in line for "Pomp and Circumstance" to start by the underclassmen making up the remains of the beloved Denton High School band, as many were graduating seniors and were not playing that night. We heard our alma mater being sung by the crowd gathered to see the elated seniors receive their hard-earned diplomas. As we had practiced, when we heard the school song end, we were to file out, staying in our present order to take our seats just as the band began to play.

We were in our places, and the diploma recipients' names were being called. Many of the students had honors that were read along with their names, and I was among them. There were some speeches, most of them short.

The audience had been requested to hold their applause until all names and honors were read. There were slightly fewer than one hundred graduates in the 1947 graduating class, and without interruption by applause, less time would be needed to get the diplomas to all graduates. As is sometimes the case, there was some applause or verbal calls that delayed the ceremony, but all in all, it went well. The speeches by some of the honored graduates were short, and suddenly, we had made it! We had our diplomas and a grand opportunity for a new beginning! Throughout the ceremony, I watched the face of my beloved, and he was smiling so proudly. He was all the family I needed there that night.

After we returned our caps and gowns and were permitted to leave, Brad and I headed for his car to make our way to my home. As is often the case after lots of excitement, I was feeling just a little let down. Brad sensed it and suggested we go out for dinner. He looked at his watch and told me that we had time, as it was only eight thirty. He knew I always had to be home before Papa left for work at ten o'clock. He headed out and told me he was taking me to Bennington's Truck Stop, where he stopped often for meals when he was on the road and the food was good. It was not too far from the high school, but it was in the opposite direction from my home.

The food was so good and such a treat for me, for other than the few band trips I had taken where the band stayed overnight, I had never eaten in a restaurant—and certainly not on a date! The waitresses in the restaurant all knew Brad, and when he told them I had just graduated, they all came and wished me well and brought us dessert on the house. With all the excitement, time got away from us.

I saw Brad look at his watch, and then he grabbed my hand and said, "Darlin', you're supposed to be already home at just this minute!"

Little good it did us to hurry, even though we did; it was 10:17 p.m., seventeen minutes late, when we arrived where he always let me out on Main Street, and by the time I walked the rest of the short distance home, I would be twenty minutes late. He left me, saying that he hoped they wouldn't be angry with me, that going out to get a snack with a friend was not unusual after someone has a big moment in their life like graduation. He left me in our usual place and drove on toward home. I guess he really didn't know my parents—and as it turned out, I didn't either! What happened next was beyond anything I could ever have imagined myself.

29

A Hint of Character

Brad often talked to me about his time in the military. I was always eager to hear his stories, for it was a part of his life that I had missed. There was one part that I will always remember, for it showed me one of many views I had of the strength of character of this man I loved. He told me of different incidents where the behavior of some of his navy buddies, while in port, was, let's say, less than exemplary.

One of the occasions was when Brad and a buddy were in one of the major deployment ports in California, where many sailors were waiting to be shipped out to parts unknown, and the major goal of his buddy seemed to be to find and be with girls—any girls—for the evening. According to Brad, this was common behavior in wartime ports, so much so that all sailors were, unfortunately, to coin a common phrase, "undesirable." And it was further made clear to them by the fact that many bars and restaurants had bold-printed signs displayed in their windows warning, "All Dogs and Sailors, Stay Out!"

On this occasion, his buddy did find a girl (Brad was still with him but had moved to a separate table with some fellows from another camp), and due to the many drinks his buddy had had, he was talking loudly. Brad could hear his part of the conversation. The girl's voice was softer, so he didn't hear her part, but he could tell by her body language that she approved of whatever her companion was suggesting. Apparently, his buddy was becoming more and more amorous to the young lady and making many promises involving plans for the future, such as wedding plans, which were seemingly being planned to take place before his ship sailed. The sailor and the girl left the bar, the sailor giving Brad and the other sailors a bold thumbs-up and a wink as they left.

Later, when Brad and his buddy were headed back to camp, Brad cautioned him that he should really think about what he was planning, saying he needed to give both of them, he and his newly found girlfriend, more time so they could get to know each other.

The sailor responded (probably thinking that Brad was just utterly naive), "You don't think that I meant any of that, do you? That was just what it took to get what I wanted, and I scored *big-time*! You should try it!"

It seems that this type of misleading behavior was prevalent among the military away from home, and Brad detested it. Hearing this made me even more proud of him.

30

An Unforgettable Night

As I arrived home on graduation night, I noticed no lights on in the house. I had a feeling of foreboding as I approached the front door. The door was locked! I never knew my mother to lock the doors; no one in our neighborhood ever locked their doors. I knocked on the door, and there was no answer, and I was beginning to get scared. I knocked again, louder this time. Still no answer!

I called out, "Mama, it's me!"

No results. I was getting more and more frightened. I went out to the sidewalk in front of the house where I could see the window of my sisters' bedroom, and both Dee and Josie were there at the window.

I asked them to come down and open the door, and they were silently shaking their heads and mouthing something to me. I finally realized what they were trying to tell me. "We can't! Mama told us we couldn't open the door, Papa's orders!"

I waited around awhile on the porch, but no one came to open the door. This was in May, and I was beginning to get quite cold; my new dress was thin, white, and very short sleeved, and it felt as if I had on nothing at all except my underwear. The only furniture on the porch was the porch swing. It was the usual slatted wooden type, and at first, I tried curling up in it to stay warm. The slats offered very little protection from the slight wind that was blowing, so I decided the wooden porch would be better, for the planks were closer together.

I curled up on the floor of the porch, and it was somewhat warmer. However, in a very short time, I was getting bitten by some sort of insect. I sat up to see what was happening, and by the glow of the streetlights, I could see that I was covered in ants! I managed to brush myself clear of them and decided the swing was my better choice after all.

I had never been so cold! My teeth were chattering. Sometime toward morning, I managed to doze off and awakened to the smell of wood smoke. My mother used thin pieces of pine as kindling to start the fire in the stove to prepare breakfast, and she rose at five thirty to start the fire in our coal-burning cook range. I knew by the smell of the kindling burning that the time was around a quarter to six, a little more than an hour before Papa returned home from work. I was so scared, for I didn't know what to expect. I hurried to the door to go in, but it was still locked. I went around to the kitchen door, and Mama was on the back porch drawing a bucket of water. When she saw me, she said, "About time you come dragging in. Just wait 'til Papa gets home!"

Threatening us with punishment from Papa was a method Mama used that always got our attention, and my gut response to her was, "I'm not waiting until he gets home. I'm leaving!" I hurried into the house and ran upstairs to my bedroom (the one where Dee and Josie were still sleeping) and grabbed my school shoes. My new white sandals were pinching my feet, and I knew I could run easier in the flat oxfords that I wore to school. I needed to borrow some money too.

On the way back downstairs, I saw my eleven-year-old sister, Shar, on a quilt on the floor in my parents' bedroom. She was awake and looking so frightened that I stopped to console her. After clinging to me for a few seconds, she seemed calmer. (She was sleeping in Mama's room, for she had just the day before had a tonsillectomy, and my mother had her there where she could watch over her in case of unexpected bleeding.) I asked her if she had any money I could borrow, for I knew that, from time to time, she ran errands for the neighbors. She couldn't speak but indicated by shaking her head that she did not, though by pointing and mouthing the words, she indicated to me that Papa's change purse was on top of the piano in the same room. It was where he usually kept it when he was home, so he must have forgotten to take it with him when he left for work. Since our family had increased so much, we no longer had a living room. The room once used for the living room was now Mama and Papa's bedroom. I went to the piano, picked up the change purse, and counted out sixty-five cents, just what he owed me. I took it over and showed it to Shar, asking her to tell him, when she could talk, that I took only what he owed me. Then I unlocked and left through the same door that had kept me locked out of a warm place to sleep the night before.

Understand that with Mama's bed being in that very room, there was no way she wouldn't have heard my pleading for her to open the door, and I have always wondered how she, a mother, felt hearing her firstborn pleading to be let in out of the chilly night air and not responding—not even to tell me she couldn't—because her husband, my father, had told her not to let me come in. I realized that Papa's word was law in that house, but if she really couldn't, did she agree that it was the right thing to do? Though I forgave my mother long ago for that night, I never forgot it. She and I never, ever talked about it.

31

The Taxi

How far could I get on sixty-five cents? I really had no plans. I only knew I couldn't stay at home any longer. I didn't have any idea what my parents would do to me. I also knew I couldn't wait to see.

I left with only the feeling of desperate need to get away. I started out for downtown by reversing my travel away from town and over the hill whose street connected with a street that I could double back on, it being the opposite way from which Papa would be coming home from work. I was formulating my plans as I ran. I took the back streets on my way downtown without really knowing what I should do or where I would go. Sometime in my mad dash to get away, I realized I had nowhere to go but to Brad. Not for a second did it dawn on me that I would be putting him in such an awkward and dangerous position.

As I was coming out on Main Street at Sinclair, a taxi was turning the corner onto Main, going south. I stopped the taxi and asked the driver how much it would cost to go to Rolling Rock; Brad's business was located there. He looked at me for what seemed like a long time and finally asked, "How much do you have?" The question puzzled me; actually, it is a better description to say that it scared me.

It ran through my mind that he may be checking in order to rob me ... but he still would only get sixty-five cents! He seemed to be thinking it over and finally said, "Get in."

I got in, and he said nothing until we were almost to the street I lived on. Then he said, "You're Becky's daughter, aren't you?"

I truthfully answered, "Yes, I am."

I did not know him, but I knew my mother had a cousin who owned a taxi service, and I asked if his name was Engle. He gave an affirmative nod, and I asked him to please not tell my mother where he took me. After a long pause, he agreed not to tell her.

Mr. Engle kept driving and seemed to be thinking about my answer. Then he said, "I know where you're going. Are you leaving home?"

Why he surmised that, I do not know. I had nothing with me except my sixty-five cents clutched tightly in my hand, no purse, not even a jacket. I still had on my white dress from the night before, somewhat mussed and possibly a little soiled from lying on the porch. Maybe he was just very astute.

"Yes," I finally answered.

He slowed the car and pulled it off the side of the road. He turned around in his seat and gently stated, "Let's talk about this just a little, huh? I think I know who you're running to, and I have no quarrel about that. Carrington's a fine fellow, but does he know you're coming?"

"No."

"What about your mother? What does she think about this?" "I don't know, but she locked me out of the house last night."

After a long silence, he finally said, "Okay, I'll take you to Rolling Rock, but I want you to think long and hard about this, and if things don't happen the way you expect them to, will you go back home?"

Going home was not anything I ever thought I'd want to do, but I saw he needed a yes, so that's what I said.

He said nothing further on the trip to Rolling Rock. Just before I got out of the car, he wished me good luck. I got out, attempted to hand him my money, which he refused, saying, "Keep it. You may need it." He waited to make sure someone came to the door of the restaurant because it was not yet open; it was probably around seven in the morning. He left when he saw me go in.

32

A Problematic Surprise

Brad's cook, Fredrick, who lived in the back of the restaurant building, had seen me once before, and he recognized me. He opened the door and let me in. I did not realize I was cold, but I was shaking all over. It was probably nerves. He went to his room and brought back blankets and put them around my shoulders and suggested I lie down on a couch in the pool hall, which was next door to the restaurant. He said it was time to open the restaurant and Brad would be there around ten o'clock, but the pool hall didn't open until eleven, and I wouldn't be disturbed before then and I should try to sleep. After the night I had spent, I really needed to; I just didn't know it showed.

Apparently I had slept soundly for some time when I was awakened by someone squeezing my hand.

I was confused and trying to figure out where I was when a calm, sweet voice I recognized asked, "Sweetheart, what happened?"

I immediately started to cry. Brad pulled me to him and found his handkerchief for me. His gentleness and the comfort of his shoulder served to completely break the dam. I'm not one for tears, generally, but this time was different. I finally pulled myself together and wiped my face on his clean white handkerchief and began to tell him my story. He did not interrupt me.

When I was finished, he was quiet for a moment and then said, "You did the right thing—the only thing you could do, I guess. But what am I going to do with you?"

Then, with his plan formulating as he talked, he began to tell me about his working schedule for that day, Memorial Day. In our part of the country, it was a day for family reunions where people gathered to honor their dead. It involved church services and grave decorating, and it was observed by most people, especially rural people. Because of that, his taxi service had been contracted for the day, which was to start in less than forty-five minutes. It was obvious he was thinking on his feet all the while he was talking to me.

Then he said, "Give me just a minute to run across the way to Wyley's [an electrical contractor who had his business across the highway from Brad's restaurant]; he has a telephone, and I need to call the people who have contracted me for the day."

As he was leaving, I heard him give his cook some kind of order, and I went to a mirror I saw in the corner over a washbasin to see if I could repair my appearance.

Brad was back in just a few minutes, and as he was coming in the door, Fredrick brought me a plate of ham, biscuits, and scrambled eggs. I realized then how hungry I was. Brad then began to tell me our plans for the day.

33

One Day at a Time

The contract for the day involving Brad's taxi service was for a family of four, and they had assured him that would leave room for me. Brad told me that the family said they would be happy to have me as part of their activities (Brad had already been included, as he would be with them all day, as per his contract). He had brought me a sweater (it belonged to his sister Treena, who had left it in his car). I was glad to have it, since I was still cold and it would help to cover a long black smudge I had noticed on the left shoulder on the back of my dress. He also had found a toothbrush for me in a little sundry sales area he had in his restaurant. I was good to go. It seemed he had taken care of this day. What then?

We drove to a small town of Grant's Lick near Waltersburg to meet the family with whom we would spend the day. We went with them to a memorial service at their church and to the graveyard on the church grounds to decorate the graves, and then we returned to their home for a family dinner. The meal they had prepared was excellent and plentiful—have I mentioned how I love to eat? They were such pleasant people and made me feel very welcome. Even under the circumstances, I enjoyed the day tremendously. I was glad to be busy; that way, I didn't have to think. One day down. What comes next?

34

Another Piece of the Puzzle

At the end of the day, Brad took me to his mother's home, where they quickly solved the problem for my night's abode. I stayed at their closest neighbor's home and slept in (or maybe I should say under) my first goose-down bed (I fought that goose all night; I thought he was trying to smother me!). It was not really that bad; I was just not accustomed to a featherbed.

Brad's mother, Alene (she suggested I call her Ma, as everybody else seemed to, neighbors as well as her family), came over after me for breakfast at seven the next morning. And what a breakfast! She had fried rabbit, eggs, gravy, and biscuits with home-churned butter and an assortment of home-canned jams and jelly on the table waiting. She had set three plates, and noticing that Brad's car was not there, I wondered who was to join the two of us. I soon learned it was just to be the two of us, that the younger brother and sister who lived there had already eaten and had gone "up the road," according to Ma. She told me Brad's father and Daniel were working near Waltersburg and were staying in that area and that Brad had gone to see one of his friends and would be back soon; then he would eat.

We had just begun to eat when Brad returned and said to me, "I think we might have worked out our little problem of finding you a place to stay." And he proceeded to tell me what he thought we could do. He said he had toyed with the idea earlier but didn't want to mention it until he had talked first to his friend to be certain it was still an option.

35

A Safe Haven; Suppressed Misery

As it turned out, Brad's friend's parents-in-law were both disabled and were raising two of their grandchildren. They needed help. What they needed, primarily, was a companion for the two grandkids, ages six and eight. The position also included giving some assistance in the kitchen and so on, but most of the time, it would be just playing with the kids. For that service, they were willing to give me room and board, and they said I would be treated like family. They suggested I try it for a week, and if it worked out, I could stay all summer. I could start right away. I thought it was a wonderful idea and told them so.

The Holts were an older couple; I hesitate to even guess their ages, but they were obviously disabled. Mrs. Holt could barely walk, and her husband was said to have a serious heart condition. They seemed very glad to have me there and kindly welcomed me to their home. The couple introduced the children to me, and they seemed well behaved and friendly. While spending that evening with the Holts, the emotion I picked up from both the older couple and the kids was relief! I don't know what they had before, or maybe it was what they saw in me that was better than what they expected.

The Holts laid out what they expected my role to be, and it included very few actual chores; most of what I had to do was to be with the kids. Other than that, washing the dishes and cleaning the kitchen were the jobs she wanted me to do for her and maybe help a little in the meal preparation, like washing and peeling vegetables. Mr. Holt asked that I do one job for him, and that was keep the water bucket filled. He was quick to say that it wasn't as easy as it sounded, for the well was eighty-five feet deep. My grandmother's well was sixty-five feet deep, and I had no trouble with that. Drawing the water turned out to be the job that caused me the most trouble, but I never let them know. Being companion to the kids was play ... literally!

The time spent with the Holts was pleasant, and the problems I had did not come from them. I did everything in my power to keep them from knowing what was happening. From the first day I was there, I realized how very tired I felt, and I was concerned about the fast rate of my heart after the slightest exertion. I constantly had to sit down. Drawing the well water was nearly impossible, but I made it by drawing a few feet, anchoring the chain back on its hook and resting, and then repeating that process until I got the water up and into the water bucket. The chain was anchored many times before one bucket was drawn. I never let the Holts know that.

Another problem that gave me grief was that Brad came so seldom during the time I was there. I had all kinds of misgivings about that. During the first week, he came twice. He came once during the second week, and the third and fourth he didn't come at all. I even gave excuses for him when the Holts would wonder and ask. (They were especially kind during his prolonged absence.) They lived some distance off the road, and one could see a car for a distance of about two hundred feet on the highway before it reached the Holts' driveway. The driveway was about three hundred feet long with some of that space hidden under a hill, so a car could be observed before it reached the driveway and most of the way up to the house. Every night, I sat on the porch and watched for him. Very few cars came by on that road, and none of them turned off during those two weeks. Having no way to communicate with him made it so bad. He was my soul mate. Time passed so slowly that summer. My physical problem did not improve; in fact, I believe it was worse in the latter weeks I was there.

I arrived there on May 31, and by July 1, I didn't know how much longer I could stand not knowing why Brad was not coming. Had he deserted me? The last time he had seen me, he seemed to be missing me as much as I was missing him, and he was so sweet. How could he act like that and then do this to me? *Oh,* I thought one evening while I sat on the porch, *here comes a car. I think it's slowing down. Oh, it is! Could it be him? Oh* no*! It's not turning! I had so hoped, but it's not him. Brad, where are you? Surely, you are not missing me like I am missing you or you would be here! Dear God, give me some kind of sign ... what should I do?*

36

Blessed News

During the next day or two, time passed a little faster because the Holt house was filled with excitement and I was busier than normal. The Holts' son was coming for the Fourth of July and would stay a few days. Mrs. Holt was preparing a feast for her son and his girlfriend, and everything had to be just right. She let me help her with the preparation, and she liked my ideas. She made me feel more useful. *I wish I didn't feel so tired!* On July 3, early in the afternoon, I was sitting on the front porch shelling peas, and I saw a car slowing down to turn into the drive. Even though it was earlier than his letter said they would be arriving, I thought it might be Charles, the son for whom the Holts were waiting. I rose to go in to tell them.

Suddenly, I realized I was familiar with that car. It was Brad's! I hurriedly put the pan of peas on the table and rushed out to meet him. The car stopped, and a familiar head poked out the driver's door, but it wasn't Brad; it was Daniel. First, I felt disappointment, and then I was alarmed. *What's happened to Brad?* Daniel saw the alarm and immediately reassured me that everything was all right.

"Brad is in Cincinnati and has been there since June 25. In the last two weeks before he left, he sold his business and cleared out anything that would hold him here and went to Cincinnati to find work. He sent word that he has a job and has found an efficiency apartment for himself and one for you if you want to come to Cincinnati. He's hoping you will, and he believes you will want to—enough that he has bought you a ticket on the train leaving tomorrow morning for Cincinnati. It would need to be tomorrow, for—being a holiday—he can meet you, for he won't have to work."

By then, I was jumping up and down, saying, "Yes! Yes! Yes!"

I heard a squeal of joy coming from behind me and turned to see the Holts were on the porch, all smiles.

Mrs. Holt, looking so happy for me, came to me and gave me a big hug, saying, "Now you will get better. I think you have just been lovesick! We are so glad for you!"

I was concerned about leaving them with such little notice, but she assured me that everything would be fine; they believed that their son and his girlfriend would be getting married and that the kids would go to live with them.

Mrs. Holt exclaimed, "I think that is the reason our son is coming home this holiday weekend, and just in case, what we have planned is a wedding!"

The next day, true to his promise, Daniel was there at the time he had stated to take me to the railroad depot and put me on the train to Cincinnati. Earlier in the day, Charlie Holt had arrived and had given his parents and his children the news Mrs. Holt expected; he was to be married and would be taking his children to Cincinnati to live with him and his new wife, Beth. They all seemed quite happy with Charles's news. It seemed to be working out well for the Holts as well as for me.

Before I boarded the train, Daniel hugged me and said, "Good luck, little sister. My big brother is sure crazy about you!"

That was so encouraging.

37

A Journey to Lost Days

I wasn't new to Cincinnati; I had been there three times before, but never alone, and being alone, the terminal seemed so strange and so big! It was filled with holiday travelers rushing madly about.

I was so scared. I thought, *There's no way I can find Brad in here.* I was panic stricken, but I really had no need to worry, because he found me. I don't even remember how we got to our apartments, for he had no car; it was at home in Kentucky. I can't imagine how I walked, for I was so weak.

I liked the neat little apartment; he had even stocked the refrigerator for me. After spending a little precious time with my beloved, just catching up, he suggested we go for a walk. I felt like it would take too much effort just to walk across the floor. I just wanted to go to bed. He thought I was just tired from the trip, so he left so I could go to bed.

The night was filled with strange nightmares. I couldn't get warm, and I felt so tired the next day. I stayed in bed and only got up to go to the bathroom and to eat a few raisins and some crackers. Sometime during the day, the landlady (she had told me I could call her Liz) came to the door and knocked. She told Brad she did but that no one had answered the door. I didn't know she was there. The day was just a daze to me. Sometime after he got home from work, Brad brought Liz over to see me. She seemed concerned and told me I should see a doctor. Seeing a doctor was almost unheard of in my growing-up years, so I told her I just needed a rest and that I had been working hard. It was not true, of course, but it put her off the subject. I heard her tell Brad that she would look in on me the next day.

I don't know how many days I was sick; it was all just a haze, but the landlady said it was four. They were days of which I don't remember the beginning or end, night or day. Brad was sometimes there, sometimes not, and Liz was coming in and leaving. I woke up one day and knew I was awake and not dreaming, and then I realized I didn't recognize the room and thought I must have just forgotten how it looked.

The next time Brad came in, I told him the room looked so different, and he asked, "Different from what?"

I said, "From when I came from the train station yesterday."

Then he told me that the day I had come to Cincinnati was almost a week before and that he and Liz had moved me into this room and that it was *his* apartment. He told me they moved me because I was too sick to stay alone. He also told me that when I got better, I would just need to say the word, and he would move me back.

The next morning, even though I was much better, my mouth had broken out in a horrific rash, and eating was difficult. The landlady had, with Brad's permission, gotten me an appointment with her doctor, and Brad took me in to see him. Again, I don't remember how I got there; I don't believe I could have walked. The doctor informed us that he believed the rash was probably caused by high fever, and he gave me a bottle of liquid that tasted suspiciously like peroxide and cost five dollars. In those days, that was a high-priced bottle of peroxide, but it worked!

Just so you know, I never did say the word! I remained in Brad's apartment, for I just didn't want to be alone, and being with the one I loved was most comforting.

Doctors I have had throughout my adult life believe that I had rheumatic fever at some time during my childhood because of signs throughout my body—specifically, my heart. I have never described this illness to these doctors, however, but it is the only suspicious ailment I have ever had and the longest lasting. All in all, I have been extremely healthy except for COPD (primarily bronchial asthma), which was diagnosed in my early seventies.

38

Needing More Room

I slowly improved and finally started regaining the weight I had lost as my appetite improved. My mouth had healed, and I was eating well, so I felt I was ready to look for a job. Everywhere were Help Wanted signs. I longed to feel like I was carrying my own weight, and to do that, I needed to find a job. It was near the end of August when Brad finally agreed that I was recovered enough to look for one. But first, before job hunting, Brad suggested we find a larger place to live. Our apartment was a studio apartment (back then, they called such unit's kitchenettes or efficiencies), and it was completely furnished but very small. I had mentioned to Brad that I would like to purchase a sewing machine with my first paycheck. As our unit was already overcrowded, he thought that if we had a larger unit, we would have room enough for a sewing machine. I agreed to look for another apartment, for I wanted to make my own clothes and would need the sewing machine to do so. I was still very thin and could find no clothing that fit, and I needed clothes for job hunting. Our landlady had larger, one-bedroom apartments in our building, but none were available at that time, so we started the tedious job of looking for a new place to live.

We walked until I didn't think I could take another step! We looked at so many apartments, many in such sorry states of repair and filthy conditions. It made us greatly appreciate Liz, our landlady, in our first apartment.

After a long, fruitless day of looking, Brad talked to a neighbor (he also worked with Brad on the railroad), who told us about a house out beyond the Western Hills Viaduct on River Road, which meant it was some distance to have to go to get to city-located jobs. But it was on the bus line and not too far from Brad's job on the railroad. The house was owned by a widow who rented out part of her space in order to help her pay her bills. It seemed that she had her own apartment on the ground floor and an open, full-size, one-bedroom, partially furnished apartment on the second floor; the third apartment was a fully furnished, rented kitchenette on the top floor. The two upper rentals had separate entrances off the same outside flight of stairs. (The owner's entrance was on the same side of the house, situated just a short distance before the entrance to the stairs leading to the second- and third-floor apartments. I mention this because everyone coming to or going from one of these apartments had to pass the owner's door.)

Our neighbor gave us a good description of the area and apartment. He was familiar with it, for as he told us, his sister and her husband had lived there before buying a house. When our neighbor told Brad about the apartment, he had mentioned that the landlady was pretty nosy—"Like most old ladies who live alone." Can't say we weren't forewarned!

We got the information we needed from him and made arrangements to see the open unit; we liked it immediately. The location had a great view of the Ohio River from the front bedroom/living-room windows. The kitchen area, on the back of the house, was small and rather dark because of the very large trees and the hill which rose steeply and abruptly behind the house. On top of the hill was a very large, heavily forested city park (we were told it was Eden Park). This was a welcome sight for us, being from the eastern area of Kentucky where forests were plentiful. (We had missed the rural setting, living in the city.) On the weekend, we could hear music and laughter from the park, and it sounded inviting.

Even though Brad had begun to do some overtime and was working some Saturdays, we thought we would still be able to do some leisure activities and hopefully be able to go up to the park some evenings or on Sunday. It didn't happen.

39

The Move

We moved in on Saturday, August 2. We had very little to move, for we were coming from a furnished studio apartment. Even though I was recovering speedily from my illness, I was still very weak, so I was not a lot of help to Brad in getting our personal items to the house. The man who had told us about the new apartment had a pickup truck, and he offered to lend it to us, but Brad did not like to borrow anything and turned down the offer. The coworker then told Brad that he would move us, and Brad, after getting him to agree to take ten dollars, took him up on his offer. It took us about an hour total to get moved; most of that time was taken by the two trips it took to walk from where we had to park at our new apartment on River Road up seventy-five steps to the first level of the house and around to the back entrance to another fifteen steps up to our apartment! (I only made it once, and Brad and his friend did the rest. I was glad we weren't moving furniture there!)

The landlady had stopped us when we were coming in with the first load to tell us to wait until we finished moving in to pay the first month's rent. Brad had only made a ten-dollar deposit when he contracted with her for the apartment. We both went down to her apartment (I hadn't yet met her).

She seemed very nice as she welcomed us to her property and suggested we grab a bite to eat and rest up for a while. Then she said, "Then, if you don't mind, I need a little help with a chore I have to get done. I would really appreciate the help." Little did we know, but the moment we agreed, our future with her was sealed!

40

Upping the Ante

We quickly ate a sandwich and went back downstairs to help our landlady in her need. Lying across the walkway between where our steps ended and the back entrance of her living quarters lay an assortment of garden tools, and among them was a shovel, some sort of digger, a grass scythe, and hedge clippers, along with several smaller cutting tools. She appeared from the front of the house with a wheelbarrow and stopped by the tools. When she stopped, as she wiped perspiration from her face, Brad asked if she wanted him to load the tools into her wheelbarrow.

She nodded an affirmative and stated, "Then take it to the bottom of the hill, please," indicating a path just around the corner of the house that went down through the grass to the bottom of the steps, ending even with the center of the front of the house. I noticed how high the grass was and wondered how it could be mowed on that steep hillside. I was soon to find out!

Our landlady (I had learned her name was Mrs. Samuels) walked halfway down the steps and asked me to come down to her level so she could show me what to do. I walked down to where she was, and she handed me a pair of garden shears and told me to start clipping the "creeper" off the step, indicating what I now know is a ground cover called crepe myrtle. It had grown in from the sides of the concrete steps, leaving about an eighteen-inch space in the middle of each step.

She indicated how much of the growth she wanted taken off by saying, "Cut it all until you come to the end of each step, both ends."

I started cutting, and after about ten minutes, I was beginning to believe that the step didn't have an end! It did, and that's when I realized that each step was six feet long by about ten inches deep, times seventy-five steps! I was to work downward and throw the scrap to the wheelbarrow that Brad had taken to the bottom of the steps.

I noticed there were around thirty steps below me. It had taken me about fifteen minutes to cut one end, and I thought maybe I would get faster as I got the hang of it. I did after about the third step, but then, a little farther down, I started slowing down, as the bending and stooping had started my back and shoulders to ache. I noticed she had given Brad a shovel and a tool that he called a mattock and had him digging out hedges at the bottom of the steps. He had done a lot of this kind of work, so he was progressing much better than I was. He had emptied his wheelbarrow several times into a dug-out area the lady had indicated as a place for the scraps.

When I finished the tenth step, I told Brad I had to quit, for my back wouldn't take any more punishment that day.

He said, "We're both going to quit! Nothing was said about this being part of our rent, and we're paying enough. I don't mind helping an older person a little when it is needed, but I'm afraid we're going to be expected to put out free labor whenever she wants things done. And just look at this place; there's a lot to be done! She told me that, when I finish digging out all the hedge, she wants me to cut the grass. I told her it was pretty steep for a lawnmower, and she said she knew that and I would be using this grass whip and scythe." He indicated two of the tools he had taken down in the wheelbarrow. "I'll finish the two remaining hedges, and that's it!"

41

Trouble Signs

I looked around for Mrs. Samuels and saw that she was sitting on her front porch with a fan and what looked like lemonade in a frosty glass. I looked down at my dress, one of the only two I had, and saw that I had grass stains on the hem and on the hip and stomach area where my arms, which were covered in grass stains, had rubbed the garment.

"That's it!" I proclaimed loudly. And then I said to Brad, "I'm going in to take a shower and see if my dress will come clean. Don't stay long, please. When you come in, I'll fix us something cold to drink."

As I went up the steps, I noticed the porch swing was empty. I was glad; I was too angry for a confrontation with her. I felt we were being used.

I was glad the next day was Sunday so that we could rest. When I awakened on Sunday morning, I was so sore that moving only slightly was agonizing. Brad didn't complain. I was to learn that Brad was quite accustomed to hard labor, and he never complained about hard work. In fact, my Brad just never complained.

We needed eggs before I could make breakfast, and Brad said he had seen a small grocery a little more than a block away when we had come into the area the day before; he would go get some eggs and whatever else I needed. Since we were going to do some major shopping at the end of next week, I thought what we had would last until then.

When I saw Brad coming toward the long flight of steps out front, I quickly put some slices of bologna on to fry (he loved fried bologna; he called it Kentucky steak). I thought I had timed it about right so that I would be ready to drop the eggs into the hot skillet right after he brought them in. Five minutes went by, and he didn't come. Then ten minutes had passed and then twenty. I looked out windows on the front and the side of the house where the walk went around, but I could not see him. I went downstairs, and at the door of our landlady's quarters, I saw his grocery sack with the eggs in it, but no Brad.

I went to Mrs. Samuels's door, and she came to the door to tell me she was having refrigerator trouble and she had stopped Brad and asked him to look at it. I could see him with the refrigerator door open doing something at the small freezing compartment at the top. She said she had to get back because she was holding the light for him but that she would send him home as soon as she could. She told me that I shouldn't worry, for he was "in good hands."

After about an hour, he came home and told me he had found that the freezer thermostat had been set at such a high setting that the temperature couldn't get low enough to freeze ice. He said the only way it would get there was for someone to turn it there, and since she had ice earlier and was the only person in the residence, she had to be the one who had readjusted it ... and he couldn't understand what she would have to gain by doing that! Also, he told me Mrs. Samuels informed him she wanted us to finish the job we had started the day before by the end of the day ... Sunday! He had told her it was impossible, that I still wasn't completely back to par health-wise and needed the day to rest and that Sunday was that—a day for resting! He also had expected to take the day off.

42

A Start of Uncertainty

One of the reasons we had moved into the bigger unit on River Road was that we could add to the sparse furnishings, if need be, and would have room for an upright sewing machine so that I could make some dresses for myself. I planned to start work soon, and I only had two dresses. One of them had gotten grass stains on it and I hadn't been able to get the stain out. I mentioned this to Brad as we were relaxing on that Sunday afternoon. He said it would just be something more we would have to move if we should decide not to stay, and he thought we should wait to see how things went.

"I know it's just been a day and a half in our new apartment, but I am not sure I want to stay where we are. What do you think about it?" he asked.

I wasn't happy with the landlady and her constant calling on Brad to look at some problem or other, especially in her apartment, and I didn't like the hard work she had started asking both of us to do. She was acting as if we were expected to do it, as if it was some kind of further payment required beyond our rent. As no such additional requirement had been mentioned, and it was not a part of our signed contract, we should not have been expected to continue in that way.

I told him, "I understand and agree, but I could go ahead without a machine and sew a dress by hand if we could buy the materials."

We had tried to get dresses to fit me, but we just could not get the right size since I had gotten so thin. He said that if I would tell him what I needed to get to make the dress, he would get them in Cincinnati after work the next day. I sent him to a dry goods store that we had seen on one of our walks in downtown Cincinnati. I told him how many yards of a good-grade cotton fabric in a light color that I would need; I didn't want white though, as I still had unpleasant memories of my graduation dress. I could get by with white thread if the cotton was very light colored. Remembering that he was slightly color blind, especially in the green and blue shades, I didn't want him to have the problem of trying to match thread to fabric, and I encouraged him to get help from the salesgirl if he had any problem. I advised him to also ask about the weight of the thread and the size of the sewing needles he would need to buy. I would need a thimble, and we determined that, for choosing it, his pinky finger was about the size of my thimble finger. Also, I would need a good pair of dressmaking shears.

Brad seemed reluctant to bother the salesgirl about such things, but I encouraged him, saying, "They would like nothing better than helping a good-looking man decide what to buy."

I also asked him to pick up a newspaper for me as well. He wanted to know which paper I wanted—the *Post* or the *Enquirer*—and I told him whichever was biggest, for I only wanted one to use as material from which to cut patterns.

He said, "In that case, I'll just pick up one from the bus. There are always lots lying around in the seats."

Almost every day, Mrs. Samuels found a reason to stop Brad. Each day, I had timed dinner so that I could take it from the stove to the table and he would get it while it was hot, the way we both liked our dinner. Her loud, lilting "Yoo-hoo!" stopped that from happening on most days.

The day he was to bring my sewing materials was one of those days. I had done up everything early, had supper just ready to put on the table, and I expected him to be at least half an hour later, because of his stop at the dry goods store, and I had timed it well. But I was holding my breath listening for his footsteps on the stairs when the dreaded "Yoo-hoo!" rang out. He didn't stay long this stop. She just wanted to talk about things in general, and he told her I was waiting for what he had stopped to pick up for me, and it was something I needed right away.

He said, "I led her to believe it was something personal that I had picked up for you, and I believe she thinks it is sanitary napkins!" We had a laugh over that.

I didn't start on my dress that night; I felt like just being with my beloved and talking about our future, something we had had little time for in the past two weeks ... and that we did for a whole evening, and we heard no further "Yoo-hoos"!

43

Looming Problems

I noticed that when we were working in the yard on that first Saturday, the weeds were wet the whole time. I thought there must have been a heavy rain the day before we moved in, but I soon realized that the area was always wet. Upon discussing it with Brad, he said he thought that it may be caused by the heavy fogs coming in off the river almost every morning. It was very rare to have a morning without fog. I had also noticed that I had trouble breathing when I was inside or outside, but I thought that it was because I was almost always going down and up lots of steps, which tended to make me have problems, especially since my illness earlier in the summer.

Another fact I think worth mentioning is that Brad had a pair of black leather dress shoes that had been issued to him when he was in the navy. He rarely wore them, and one day when I was cleaning the closet floor (we had only lived there two weeks), I reached in to move his shoes, and they felt strange. I brought them out into the light and could hardly recognize them; they were covered with a dark-gray, fuzzy mold! He also had a leather notebook that held his job certifications, blueprints, and welding diagrams from his former job in the shipyards. These were brought in the event he would apply for a welding job in the Cincinnati area. The notebook was covered with the same mold as the shoes, and the pages were damp and stuck together.

44

Troublesome Issues

Both Brad and I had started having aches in our joints, and we chalked that up to our being physically out of shape from living in the city for the last couple of months and, for me, because of my recent illness. Also, Brad thought that part of my problems was that my body had to build back muscle and weight, which would take time, for it had only been a short while since I had started to recover.

He said, "Knowing how weak you must be, I don't think you should go about it too quickly, because you're still not back to normal."

I had wanted to look for a job before now, but Brad thought I should give myself a little longer so that I would have the stamina I would need to hold down a job once I was hired.

45

Trouble Brews

The subtle (sometimes not so subtle) demands from the landlady continued. When I was home alone, she did not bother me; I don't know if she even knew I was home. I was very quiet during the day, hoping that she would leave me alone, and she did. She didn't mention the yard work again and did hire a man to do some of it. However, her demands of Brad's time continued. There was no way he could get to our steps without passing her back door where she would stop him with "just a little something" for which she needed his help. He went around the opposite side of the house one evening in an attempt to avoid her by approaching the steps without passing her door. No such luck! She saw him through her kitchen window on the back of the house and stopped him anyway. That day was a Friday, and Brad didn't want our weekend tied up and was afraid if she stopped him that day, it was likely to happen, for it was not easy to say no.

This time, when our landlady stopped Brad, she was all sweet and gracious, saying she was having her car brought around for us to use to bring in some bulky groceries that she knew we must need by now.

Mrs. Samuels said, "You have already been here three weeks and have brought very little in. Of course I will go along with you and get some needed items myself, so that way, you won't feel bad taking my car."

Mrs. Samuels suggested going to Findley Markets to get some fresh fruits and vegetables and maybe some meat. "They have wonderful chicken and fresh as well as smoked pork," she told us.

She also recommended a large grocery store in the same area. I had heard good things about the Findley Markets in downtown Cincinnati and wanted to experience shopping there, so it didn't sound like a bad idea. Mrs. Samuels apparently needed to have someone drive for her, and we could get our own groceries as well. Sounded like a fair exchange.

Brad drove her car to the Findley Markets area, but no parking was permitted anywhere close to the Markets, so after our leaving her off at a meat market inside Findley and after finding parking, there was yet a distance to walk to get back to the market area. That was okay, for it was only about three and a half city blocks. Walking that distance while carrying lots of groceries, fruits, and vegetables, however, was going to be a little difficult.

When we returned to Mrs. Samuels at the meat market, she had already bought several packages of meat along with a whole chicken (including the feet) and a hog's head (which both made bulky, hard-to-carry packages). One of the items I needed was potatoes, and Findley had tremendous prices on twenty-pound bags. I didn't want that much, but I needed potatoes, and Brad encouraged me to go ahead and buy a bag, for they should keep long enough for us to use them. I put them in the cart while looking at all the other items already there and keeping in mind that the cart could not be taken out of the market and that we must carry what we bought back to the car.

Our decision to buy the potatoes prompted Mrs. Samuels to get a bag as well. I was shocked at what was going into the cart, and I started to warn her we had to be able to carry what we bought. Brad knew what I was going to say and shook his head, mouthing, "It's okay." He did, say, however, that we had about as much as we could carry and that we had better start getting it back to the car, hoping she'd take the hint.

The very next booth was a fruit stand, and they had just brought in bushel baskets of southern-grown peaches. We could buy them by the bushel or half bushel, but if we didn't want that much, they were sold by the pound. The per-pound price, though, was considerably higher, as the kiosk's sign indicated. We wanted some just to eat fresh, so I bought ten pounds, thinking that I could carry the ten pounds along with Mrs. Samuels's smaller packages of meat, and, as I told her, we would share them with her. Since we were back where we bought the potatoes, I also asked the man in that kiosk to put my twenty-pound bag into two smaller mesh potato bags I had seen there. Then, hopefully, Mrs. Samuels could carry one ten-pound sack of potatoes, and I could carry the other along with her packages of meat. That would leave the hog's head and Mrs. Samuels's twenty-pound sack of potatoes for Brad to carry.

When Brad saw I was to carry two grocery sacks and the second mesh bag of potatoes, which would amount to about thirty pounds or more, he grabbed the ten pounds of potatoes and slung them across his shoulder and said, "Now, are we ready to go?"

Mrs. Samuels stopped him, saying, "No, I want a half bushel of peaches."

I had had it with her! I had never said anything to her before about the way she had treated us like slaves, especially Brad, and had interrupted our lives the whole time we had lived there. The long pent-up feelings I had because of her irksome meddling in our lives for the past three and a half weeks—and then *this*—had brought my temper to the boiling point.

I spat out, "What do you think he is, a mule? He's already got all he can carry; I've got all I can carry! Do you intend to carry the peaches?"

She flounced off as she said, "No! And I'm not carrying the potatoes either. They're yours! Get them to the car any way you can!"

Angrily, she headed down the street in the direction of where the car was parked, a little more than three blocks away.

I picked up the potatoes she had dropped, and Brad took them from me, handing me the hog's head, saying, "It weighs less than the potatoes. I can handle them."

We began to follow after Mrs. Samuels and managed to keep just slightly behind her with our loads.

As soon as Brad got the car unlocked, she got into the front passenger's seat, her frown as dark as a thunder cloud, and when Brad asked if she wanted us to find another way home, she retorted, "You drove me down here —now drive me home!"

Brad said, "I'm not sure I want to, and the way you're acting, I'm not sure you even want me to!"

She quieted down a bit and said, "Aw, come on. We'll sort this all out tomorrow."

We got into the car and drove back to River Road.

The next day was Saturday. Earlier in the week, Mrs. Samuels had asked Brad to patch a spot on her roof where it leaked around a chimney. The man living on the top floor had complained about a leak into the closet in his unit and had asked her to have it fixed. She had asked her usual repairman to look at it, and he had told her he could not stand heights and would not go on a roof job of any kind.

This seemed like a legitimate need, and Brad was going to repair it for her, for, as he said to me, "I don't believe I'll have to worry about her climbing up there to 'help' me!"

I had all along felt certain that Mrs. Samuels's calling on Brad so much for things that seemed unnecessary and that sometimes were even trumped-up reasons was because she just wanted his attention. He had begun to feel uneasy because she always wanted to stand too close to him when he was trying to determine the cause and come up with the solution of the problem for which she had stopped him. Too many times she had "accidentally" bumped up against him as she held a light for him or steadied a board or assisted him in other—many times unneeded—ways. And not many days went by without her stopping him on his way home from work to get him to check something for her or just to get his opinion on something.

On Saturday, Brad gathered his tools and the materials Mrs. Samuels had gotten for him to do the roof job. He set up ladders that Mrs. Samuels had borrowed for the job and climbed to the roof. It took him about forty-five minutes before he felt satisfied that the job was complete. He cleared all debris from the job, got down off the roof, and put the ladders away. He then stopped at her back door to let her know the job was done. She asked him to come in for a minute, as she needed to talk to him.

He went inside and took the offered chair, and she started immediately with what she had to say.

She began, "It was unfortunate that the scene last night had to happen, and you have just gotten caught in the crossfire. I can't ignore the fact that Rachel mouthed off in such an uncalled for, selfish, hateful way, and I will *not* ignore it. She is no longer welcome here, and I want her out of here at the end of the month. You can stay if you want to, but she has to go. It hurts me that you didn't stand up for me, for I have treated you guys like family. Thank you for repairing the roof. If you insist on leaving too, I will give your deposit back after I have inspected and made sure everything is clean and in good repair."

Brad told her that we would be out by the end of the month.

46

Search, Decision, Action

The next day, Sunday, August 24, we decided we had better get out and start looking for a place. The newspaper Brad had picked up on Friday (before we knew we would have to move) was still in our apartment, and we spread it out looking for something promising.

We saw a listing for the address where we had lived when Brad had first arrived in Cincinnati. Brad said immediately, "Why don't we go to our former landlady and check this out? It might be one of the bigger units she has; we won't know if we don't check it out!"

I heard the excitement in Brad's voice in his exclamation and thought, *Liz, our former landlady, was such a great landlady; we were so happy there, but the apartment was just too small. Wouldn't it be wonderful if she would have an open one-bedroom unit?*

Brad and I caught the first bus that came by, and it took us into the downtown bus depot where we were to transfer, getting one going up to the area of our former apartment. When we got off the bus, Brad said, "It's such a nice day. Why don't we walk?"

We had walked from near the depot numerous times when we lived there, so we started out. We had gotten less than halfway when I started having problems breathing, and my legs were extremely weak. I didn't say anything at first, and Brad noticed me sort of stumbling and wanted to know if I was having problems.

I laughed and said, "I didn't realize how out of shape I had gotten."

We started walking more slowly, and I was so happy when we were getting close to our destination. When we made it, I made a mental note not to even try walking back to the depot.

We rang the bell for Elizabeth King's apartment. I had known her the months we had lived there only as Liz. She was happy to see us and immediately asked me if I had been sick again. I told her I had found it hard to breathe where we were living and that it might have been because it was always so damp.

We told her where it was located, and she remarked, "That's a long way out of town! Do you ever think you might want to come back here?"

Brad told her, "We saw your ad, and that's why we're here. We are hoping it is one of the bigger units."

She immediately said, "It is! Would you like to see it?"

We looked at it, and after getting the specifics, we told her we would take it. It was less rent than where we were staying, and what was most exciting was she told us that we could move in immediately, for the tenant had already vacated. It was then about half past noon on Sunday. We signed the paperwork and told her we would move in as soon as we could get someone to move us.

She asked if we had bought any furniture, and Brad answered, "Fortunately not. Something just didn't feel right about that place from the start, and I put off getting any because of that feeling."

Liz said, "I've got an idea. Why not move in today?"

"With our clothes and personal items, it would be too much to bring by bus, and I have to wait and talk to one of my buddies with a truck—or just a car would be large enough," Brad replied.

As soon as Brad finished his sentence, Liz jumped up and said, "I've got another idea! I brought my car from the country and have it across the street in one of the parking spaces for this building. We could go out now and get your things and move you in here by evening. Why don't we do that?"

Brad looked at me and asked, "Can we be ready that fast?"

I had been going over it in my mind, and it looked doable. I said, "Why not? I just cleaned the whole apartment yesterday, and what little cleaning that I would have to do after packing our personal items and clothes would just amount to wiping out the drawers, the shower, and sinks and running the sweeper. Altogether, packing, loading, and all should take no more than an hour—that is, if someone else can do the running up and down the hill from the apartment to the car and back. We could probably get it all down in two to three trips though."

Liz jumped up and said, "Let me call my friend downstairs to see if she can come up and sit here until I get back. I do still have an ad in the paper, but she knows my business and can fill in for me. I am strong, and I will help you load the car."

She took care of the call, her friend arrived almost immediately with her knitting in tow, and we were good to go.

When we had everything loaded, Brad stopped at Mrs. Samuels's door to tell her we were moved and to ask her for his deposit of ten dollars back. At the mention of our deposit, she began to shake her head.

Brad asked if there was a problem, and she immediately said, "Our agreement was for you to move at the end of the month!"

Brad replied, "Our rent is paid until the first of next month, and I am not asking for that back; I agree that I owe that, and for the days covered, you have the apartment back to do whatever you want with it. I am here for the deposit of ten dollars to be returned to me."

Finally, he got her to agree that that was fair and then suggested she might want to go look at the apartment so there would be no misunderstandings about its condition to qualify us for the deposit return. He followed her upstairs and stood while she gave the unit a close inspection. She seemed satisfied until she opened the closet door where we had found the mold. He saw her sniff the air, and she immediately said, "This closet doesn't even *smell* clean. It will cost me more than ten dollars to get someone to come in and clean it, so I can't give the deposit back."

Brad started to tell her that in that closet was where we kept finding mold and it smelled musty, for it seemed always to be damp. Stopping himself from making that statement, he thought, *What's the use arguing with her?*

He merely said, "I'm sorry you feel that way. Have a good day." Then he turned and left.

From the time we left her apartment, it was exactly one and a half hours until we were moved into apartment 202 on Republic Street, once again in the first building in which I had ever lived in Cincinnati!

47

The Dress

The dress I had made by hand, when finished, looked even better than I had expected.

When Brad had come home with my sewing materials, I hadn't known what to expect. He had chosen well, however. The fabric was a pale pink, printed with very small sprigs of larkspur in groups of three stems gathered and tied in tiny white ribbons, with this pattern repeated evenly all over the fabric. Brad had bought white bias binding for the dress (at the salesgirl's suggestion), and that gave me the idea for the finished product.

The dress, which was sleeveless, was fashioned with a mock placket edged in the smooth, crisp white of the bias binding, with the placket starting at the round neckline and then down the front to the waist. It also had a false collar of the larkspur-sprigged fabric, starting at each side of the three-inch placket opening in the back of the bodice (the opening would be closed with a button and a loop).

The mock collar followed the curve of the neckline and was sewn flat around the neckline, joining the back placket opening and the mock placket in the front. The sewn-down collar was also trimmed in the white cotton bias tape. The dress had a belt made from the pink fabric edged in white bias tape with a stiffened belt form enclosed within the fabric. The belt was to be worn with the stiffened part across the back and to come around to the front, leaving four inches between ends of the stiffener in the middle front of the dress. The material covering the belt form was made to extend eighteen inches beyond the ends of the stiffener (also edged in white) and, at that point, became sashes. The sashes were to be tied in the center front of the dress.

The skirt of the dress was mostly straight with slight tucking at the waist, allowing it to fit smoothly at the bodice and to the increasing fullness from my waistline to my hips. In the center back seam, a kick pleat was fashioned to be seven inches from top of the pleat to the hem, giving the skirt the needed fullness for a comfortable walking stride.

I was proud of that dress, partly because I had done a good job on it and partly because Brad had chosen the fabric for it and bought all the necessary trim. The only thing he did not get was the button for the back neckline fastener, but he did get the side zipper. I didn't think to tell him I would need a zipper, but he had taken my advice about getting a salesgirl to help him. As for the button, I removed a button from the very bottom of one of Brad's shirts, and that did the job. He didn't even miss the button!

48

Looking Forward

We had moved back to Cincinnati on August 24. I had wanted to start looking for a job at the beginning of the month, but I was really glad Brad held me back, as I probably wouldn't have had the stamina to hold down a job. By then, it was August 30, and I was feeling much better. I had decided to wait until after Labor Day week to hit the job market. People with whom I had become acquainted in my building had told me that there was not much chance of being hired during the Labor Day week as past history seemed to indicate. I had decided to wait until the following week.

Brad bought me a sewing machine as soon as he got paid. With this machine, I could get to work on a new dress, making the job much easier the second time. First, I had to come up with a design. But even before that, I had to get my creative juices flowing. I had a little time before I started to job hunt to make another dress. It would certainly be easier on a sewing machine. I really had only one dress that was fit to wear and one, well, not so suitable. The not-so-suitable one I had was the white eyelet dress I had for graduation, and it had gotten rather limp. I tried starching it, but that didn't do much for it. Then the dress I wore every day when I didn't go out was the one with all the grass stains on it. Then there was the new pink one I had just made.

A sewing machine would be so useful in so many ways when we had *our* house. I just couldn't wait to make curtains, slip covers, and fluffy pillows in bright, cheery colors for a home of our own.

49

Hurdles of Confusion

I had known several of my Kentucky neighbors' daughters who had gone to Cincinnati after graduating and had gotten jobs. They would return home a month or so later, flashing new wardrobes and hairdos, and they would talk (they even talked differently) about how they loved their new jobs, constantly bragging about their apartments and what they planned to do with the next paycheck ... I wanted to be there myself. Most of these girls had gotten factory jobs, so I just assumed that would be the type of work I should seek.

You will recall that, earlier, I mentioned that our little town of Denton and surrounding areas offered little to no employment for the returning military and none at all for high-school graduates without college (especially females) who were thrown on the job market, except for jobs as carhops or waitresses or cleaning personnel for the town's very few hotels/motels, the latter being reserved mostly for older workers, and the railroad, which kept its status quo and rarely needed to hire. Brad was happy I wanted to work, but he would always add, "For a while." I never thought to mention to him what type of job I planned to seek.

At the beginning of September, I felt so much better and really wanted to get started being productive. Brad agreed that I seemed pretty much back to normal.

The Monday of the week following Labor Day, I left the apartment armed with a list of ads of interest to me, the bus schedule, and lots of confidence that this was going to be a piece of cake. Because I really was not familiar with Cincinnati, I decided to go through the Ohio State Employment Office to get a better idea of what was available. As I stepped through the door, I decided if the lines were any indication, there were a lot of unemployed people in Cincinnati!

Here was my first hurdle, competing with the great numbers of unemployed. *Oh well. I can do this*, I thought. A number of long lines extended from the front of the room at a long row of desks back toward the doorway that I had come through. Some of the lines were shorter than others, so I picked the shortest one and waited.

Fifteen minutes or so later, a woman in a line beside me smiled at me and asked, "What's your name?"

Thinking she was being friendly, I answered, "Rachel." With a frown, she said, "Your *last* name!"

I told her, and she said, "You should be in that line," indicating one several lines over, one that seemed to be the longest of them all.

Why did she think I would have to go to the back of that line? Then I noticed that way up at the beginning of that line on the attendant's desk something I had not seen before—a sign indicating last names beginning with *G–J* should be in that line. All other lines had similar directives. *G* for *Gaylord*—that would be me. I had lost at least fifteen minutes and probably that many or more spaces in line ... my second hurdle. *I can do this*, I reassured myself.

It was still morning when I reached the desk labeled, "Names beginning in *G, H, I,* and *J*." *J* for Jones, maybe Johnson. Oh my! No wonder it took so long. My name fell into the category where there were lots of people under those common names! I gave my name, Rachel Gaylord, and the attendant checked her list and, not finding my name there, asked to see my social security card ... my third hurdle! I didn't have one. She explained that to work at any job, I had to have a card and that I should get one and come back. She explained that I could apply for it at another office in the building and come back and go to the back of the line when I had the card in hand. Great! The fourth one, and the hurdles were getting bigger. *If I don't hurry, I won't get to work today*!

I cleared my more-difficult-than-I-thought fourth hurdle and finally had gotten my card after hitting an age-requirement rule, for I needed to be eighteen years old before I could get a social security card. I wanted to work so badly, so I simply adjusted my birth date, as no birth certificate was required, which caused me a peck of trouble a year or so later when I went in for a social security name change. It seemed social security laws were different back then. The people manning those desks that day would probably never have believed that, one day, newborns would be permitted to have cards like those for which we were applying.

My card was issued, and I went back to the lines. I believed that, on that day, the lines may have been a little shorter, but there still must have been a lot of Johnsons and Joneses needing jobs! It was almost three o'clock when I got back to the same desk—to a different lady, however. She didn't ask for my name but jumped ahead by asking for my social security card. I proudly showed her my brand-new card, and she got down to business.

When I told her I was looking for a factory job, she looked at me with some degree of doubt evident on her face and asked, "Could I possibly interest you in another type of work, young lady? Most of the available factory jobs are looking for workers with ... ah, a bit more maturity, I believe."

When I insisted on factory work, she gave me cards with names of places looking for workers in certain listed job classifications. There were three of them. All of them were jobs running some type of machine or "line work" (whatever that was), and she had written dates and times for me to appear for interviews. I noticed one was for an Addressograph machine. I had seen pictures of the machine and had read something about them in an article I had seen back in my high-school library. That's something I could do, I decided. But all the interviews were for the following day.

"Could I get an interview for today?" I asked hopefully.

She glanced at the clock with an exasperated look and said, "Day shift is over in the factories, and they only interview during day shift. You're lucky they are for tomorrow and not next week."

I was going to have to work on that patience thing.

50

Discouraging Steps

I went home all excited about the job that I would probably get the next day. I may not have been there in patience, but my confidence soared high! Brad was tickled to see I still was hopeful after I had told him about my hurdles, but I had gotten over them, hadn't I? When he saw the job classification choices I had to try for, I think he was a little doubtful, but he said nothing to discourage me. He did give me some pointers in going through the interview process; nothing in this line had been covered in my high-school college-prep course work. He told me it wouldn't hurt to bluff just a little, if I really felt I could do the job; he then warned me to stay truthful. (How could I do both?) He encouraged me by saying that the companies would not have advertised the position as requiring no experience if they didn't plan to train the new employees, so I really had nothing to worry about. Of course not, but I probably could find something. What happened to my confidence? Maybe it soared too high and flew away!

The next day I got to the first job site early and waited in a dirty little office for over an hour. I began to be afraid they had forgotten me when one of the doors in the back of the office flew open and a small man rushed in, bringing with him a smell of something burning and lots of horrendous shrieking noise. He apologized for his lateness and explained he was trying to repair a machine whose bearings were shot. He didn't get the job done by the sound and the burning smell.

His company was hiring an Addressograph operator, he told me, and the job would start the following week. He asked if I thought I could learn the machine. I told him I was somewhat familiar with the machine and I should be able to handle the job. *There goes the bluff part.* He abruptly asked me how tall I was, and I told him, "Five foot three."

The next question was, "How much do you weigh?"

Now he was getting personal! "One hundred three," I replied.

"Honey, you'd have to wear forty-pound weights to even pull the handle on that bugger!" he exclaimed.

I insisted that I was stronger than I looked, and looking very doubtful, he asked me to come with him. We went out through the same door he had come in, past the screaming machine, and into a side door that, fortunately, would close to keep out some of the factory noise. In that room was a machine I recognized as an Addressograph from the picture I had seen; nowhere was that picture labeled "One-tenth size." The machine in that room was *huge*! The handle he had referred to was on the side of the machine. The hand grip was little more than head high to me, so I could reach it without stretching. Then he asked me to pull it down. At first, I thought it was locked in place. I put my weight to it, and it came down. *Yeah, I can do it!* I thought.

He said, "It's empty. Now let's load it." He reached to a high shelf above the machine and pulled down a box of metal plates a little smaller than wallet-card size and proceeded to fill slots in the machine.

I looked around for a stool, for I knew I could not reach the supply of plates without one. I saw none.

He typed a bit on a keyboard, closed the machine, and said, "Go ahead. It's loaded."

I was prepared to put my weight on it if I had to and grabbed the handle. My feet came off the floor, and the handle did not budge!

"I didn't think so," he said.

I was embarrassed because I couldn't do the job, and realizing that, he said, "That machine runs by electricity, generally, but the person operating it must be able to manually operate it in order to clear jams, which happen several times a day. You couldn't do it.

"I would love to have a position where I would be able to hire you, but I haven't. You have grit, and I am confident you will find something. However, thank you for interviewing."

I had missed my second interview; the first one had taken too long. My third listed interview was at a soap manufacturing plant. I was impressed by the plant and amused at their movie-type sign showing a bar of soap jumping from a diving board. The sign said something about the soap floating, never sinking. Clever!

The interviewer told me I was being interviewed for work on the "line." That told me very little. He explained that it was a production line and that each worker had to complete a specified application to the product as it moved from left to right in front of the workers. The line was set to a designated speed, and each worker was required to do his or her portion of preparing the product for the market. I was concerned about keeping up, but he assured me that the lines were set to a comfortable speed for most everybody after the worker acquired a little practice. (This interviewer was using the direct opposite approach from the one on the other interview. He was consistently telling me "You can," while the first job interviewer kept telling me "You can't!") Then, on a little scaled-down line simulator he said was set to the same speed as those on the floor, he gave me instructions and let me practice on a portion of it for a few minutes, and then he started the whole thing (a length of about ten feet of line) and let me practice. I got a little nervous and dropped some pieces and got behind, but he said I did well.

After I was finished, he sent me for my physical. I was put through a regimen of tests, and I seemed to be passing. After it was finished, two doctors were conferring, and I could see they were discussing my feet while shaking their heads. Then they told me that because of the way my shoes were worn on the soles and the uppers run over at the heels, which could indicate foot problems, they were afraid I couldn't stand on my feet the length of time required on the line. I didn't think they would believe me, but I told them, truthfully, that a neighbor had given me those shoes to wear to finish out my year in high school, that the shoes were worn like that when she gave them to me, and that they weren't comfortable. They conferred again and had me walk barefoot and observed me for some time. After having me remove my shoes and walking back and forth without them, they agreed my feet seemed okay. I was so relieved.

I only had one more test to go, and they told me I had done well so far. My last was an eye exam. One of the doctors checked my eyes, conferred with the other one, came back and did more testing, conferred again, and then examined my eyes again. Then both of them left the room. My original interviewer came back and called me into his office. He told me he had bad news for me—that I had not passed the interview because of the eye test and explained that since the company's lines ran left to right and the ability to see with my left eye appeared to be marginal, at best, they were afraid it would be a safety hazard for me to work the lines.

"I do have a suggestion, however," the interviewer said. Somehow, the suggestion for a chance at other employment that could come later did little to soften the blow of not getting the job I had hoped for.

He went on to tell me he had examined my high-school transcript and thought I would be a good candidate for their corporate offices. He told me they weren't hiring for those positions at present and that it would be early fall when hiring resumed and that I should watch for their ads. They would keep my interview and physical results on file for one year, and all I would need to do was to test for the office. I wasn't interested ... I wanted a job immediately.

Knowing what I now know, the position they had suggested I apply for when it became available was located in an area then called Ivorydale. A job with that company, a soap manufacturer, would have been a wonderful career opportunity for me—that is, *if* I had stayed in the Cincinnati area.

51

A Different Strategy

I returned to our apartment with the disappointing news that I did not get a job. Brad listened quietly while I told him about my day. Several times, he chuckled about the situation as I talked. Finally, I stamped my foot and exclaimed, "What's so funny?"

He pulled me into his arms and said, "You are, my darling, with your telling of it!"

I had to admit, the experiences I had were comical ones, a virtual comedy of errors, and we laughed together.

Then Brad very seriously asked, "Why on earth do you want to work in a factory? Wouldn't a nice clean office job suit you better?"

I guess I just assumed that working in a factory would be more in line with what he would want me to do. Apparently, he wasn't eager to see his future wife become a Rosie the Riveter. (This was a rather derogatory label applied to women who did factory work, for that type of work had, in the past, primarily been filled by men. During wartime, women had to step up to the plate to fill spots previously held by men who had been drafted or had volunteered into the military.)

The next day, I went back to the employment office. I breezed right through the lines in no time at all. I thought that I must be becoming a pro at this job-hunting process, or maybe it was because Monday could be typically busier than other weekdays. You think? Soon I had a list of three possible clerical job interviews scheduled for the following day. I went home very excited. Then I started worrying about the next day since testing might be a part of the interviews and a typing test could be a requirement.

Typing was not my strong suit in school. I was scared of my class instructor. He would sneak up from behind during a timed test and yell out a student's last name followed with "Stop looking at the keyboard!" or other admonishments, and I had not been excluded.

I could never relax during a test in his class. Consequently, my speed was rather poor. I learned from one of the school office workers some few years after I graduated that because of the poor grade I earned in that class, it had drastically brought down my grade point average. So what? I didn't want to be valedictorian ... that's a speech I didn't have to make. Public speaking was not my forte, then or now. Sour grapes? Maybe.

Because of our dear landlady Liz's ability to sense her tenants' moods and in answer to her usual greeting of "What can I do to make it all better, dear?" I confided my worries to her. She told me that, from time to time, she volunteered in the public library and knew there were typewriters there for the public's use. She suggested that I spend some time there that evening to hone my typing skills.

After Brad came home and we had dinner, I asked him to walk to the library with me to practice typing. It could just be part of our usual early evening walk. We had again been taking a couple of hours each evening to walk; it was cooler then, and we enjoyed walking hand in hand and just talking. Simply talking was becoming such a pleasure for us, and it never ceased to be one of our special pastimes throughout our life together. We always talked about everything. I still remember our talks as being the part of our lives together that was the most enjoyable leisure pastime.

52

A Repeated Plea

One topic that came up often in Brad's and my frequent long talks was my parents and how my having run away might be affecting them. This was a subject I really did not want to pursue, but my beloved was rather persistent. I was still angry with them. I even somehow blamed them for my illness, for I connected it with the cold exposure I had experienced the night I was locked out. Whether that was a factor or not, we will never know. Oh, I don't blame them now, and that subject never came up with them in all the years they lived afterward. To them, it was as though it had never happened, though I didn't forget it. It seemed to be indelibly stamped in my mind.

Brad's purpose for bringing up the subject of my parents was to try to get me to see, as he would say, "where they're coming from." I believe his being more mature than I was and a parent himself gave him more insight into the situation than I had with my miniscule amount of life experience. He suggested I write to them and let them know I was okay. I guess my attitude was to just let them worry. Looking back, the reason was I really wanted to punish them.

At that point, Brad, interrupting my tirade, said, "Honey, your parents are pretty certain you are with me. It isn't just because you have run away and they don't know where you are that they worry; it probably is because *they believe you're with me.*"

I didn't want them to have the comfort of knowing I was okay and happy. I am not a cruel person, but I was really angry. What my wise friend had said then puzzled me greatly until another time when I allowed him to bring up the subject.

He then said, "Oh, but your being with me *is* the real problem!"

Brad continued to bring up the subject of my parents. In one of these conversations, he started to point out more in depth the situation of my being away from home and the worries my parents were experiencing, and he encouraged me to try to see it from their point of view.

He went on to say, "Your parents don't know me. What they do know is that I am a married man and am much older than their teenage daughter. And to them, possibly, the fact that I love you isn't something they would readily believe. I'm sure they believe I talked you into leaving, or they may even believe I *forced* you to go with me.

"Your parents feel that I have no right to you. They don't know I love and want the best for you. They will have the influence of my wife and her people making it look as if I am having a fling while she is at home having to raise our family alone. She probably thinks I'm just having a ball, running around without any responsibilities at all. My own family lives some distance from Denton, and her people live in or very near Denton. Her family members are the ones spreading the half truths your parents will hear, and I believe that's what they are hearing. Most people know nothing about the pending divorce and what led up to it; they will only know what they hear from Bobbie's family, and unless they know me well, they will believe what they hear. Those who really know me won't be heard by the people in Denton, for I'm not from Denton. I know the Dawson family, and I know they hurt for their daughter and their sister, and they will be vicious. Your family will hear and believe all this. She is there, and I'm not. She will point out what is evident, and I can't fend for myself, and at this point, I don't have a legal leg to stand on. My not having a divorce and living as if we were married is *not* legal; in fact, it is against the law for me, because you're a minor, and to be with you, I am forced to protect myself by hiding.

"The last few weeks we were in Denton—remember, you were at the Holts'—I felt I was being followed and was fearful that maybe someone had been hired by your parents to find you. I couldn't risk leading them to you, and I avoided coming to see you myself. I decided then that I would just sell out, leave the area, and go somewhere I felt we'd be safe until I could legally claim you as my wife. Think about this, and don't blame your parents!

"In the meantime, please write to them, and tell them you are okay and that you're not blaming them—if this is something you think you can do. Don't give away where you are. I have a friend who will mail your letter from another state, so the postmark won't lead them to us."

I did send one letter through Brad's friend just to let my parents know that I was doing well. I was to learn that it had thrown some doubts about where I was staying. My mother told me they had believed I could be in Cincinnati, that being the usual city that those leaving home from our area headed. My letter coming from the Louisville area caused them to doubt their Ohio theory.

I later told my parents they didn't know what a friend and supporter they had in my beloved Brad. Part of the parental guidance and training I acquired while still a teenager came not from my parents but from my then husband-to-be, later my loving husband. Stockholm syndrome as one of my twice-divorced, man-hating so-called friends dared to suggest once. No way! My relationship with this wonderful man was never anything but wholesome.

53

The Job Interview

I felt my typing practice had gone well, as I had ended my practice session at the library with a time of sixty words per minute, much better than I had ever done in class. Brad had kept the time for me as I did the test, and he gave me no pressure. His kind, gentle voice calling out time was the only interruption I had during the tests, and I felt no stress with him. The same was not true during the required test at my job interview the following day through no fault of those interviewing me, as they really put no pressure on me. Stress is part of my makeup. Consequently, my own self-made stress chopped off ten words per minute of my score, but the company seemed quite happy with my fifty words per minute.

The first interview was with an insurance company on Fourth and Main Streets in downtown Cincinnati. I liked the area. I noticed a number of stands selling sandwiches, small hole-in-the-wall restaurants, and even a high-end restaurant or two where I could go for lunch on the rare occasion I would eat out if I managed to get a job with the insurance company. In riding the bus to the address, I also saw that an area familiar to me, Fountain Square, was close by, a place where Brad and I had visited on our long evening walks.

The interview at the insurance company and the testing (timed typing, a combination of math and essay writing, and a multiple-choice test which, I believe, was compiled to determine what an applicant's reaction would be to certain situations) went quite well. I thought the test was extremely simple and decided I must be missing the concept of what they really wanted, which scared me for a moment. Then I remembered that I had two more job possibilities if I did not make it on my first try.

That thought calmed me. I remember the instructions for the writing part of the test clearly, asking me to write a short essay in eighty words or less about why I wanted the job. Even though I have no memory of even the essence of what I wrote, I clearly remember the "eighty words or less" part of the instructions. I had wondered if I didn't get eighty words in my reason. How many less than eighty would they consider enough? (Have you picked up on the fact that I may be a worrywart?) Brad had said to me many times, "Honey, you worry too much." I wrote and rewrote the short essay three times before I was happy with it. I still had plenty of time left. When I was satisfied that it contained enough but not too many words, I decided to use it. But by counting the words again, I'd be more certain. (There's a name for that sort of behavior.) I had exactly eighty words! I recopied it onto the test form and handed my paper to the interviewer, who had just come back into the room. There were two of us in the room taking the test that day, and I had been told there was only one position being filled. The other person was still busily writing. That gave me some concern. Had I missed the concept after all?

A short time later, I was called into the interviewer's office. He sat in a chair beside the desk with a stranger in his former seat behind the desk. Both gentlemen stood as I took the chair offered me. The gentleman behind the desk leaned across and extended his hand, saying, "Miss Gaylord," and then introduced himself as president of the company. He continued, "I'd like to offer you the job of claims clerk of the Southwest Indemnity Insurance Company, if you would like to have it. May we put you on the payroll?"

I was ecstatic! My first job! I could not wait to get home to tell my beloved. I knew he would be so happy for me. I saw no more of the other interviewee. Maybe she was still back there writing.

The company president then took me into an adjoining office where several girls sat at workstations, and he introduced me around. I found out later that I was younger than all the others. I hoped that would not make a difference in the way they would treat me. It seemed that there were two other girls who had the same job classification as mine. A third woman was older, one whose nameplate declared her "Supervisor of Claims." She was introduced as our supervisor. Lastly, I met one other, whose position was switchboard operator/receptionist, and she was introduced as one who would "pick up the slack" when she had spare time and the claims girls had overloads. I was told this was bound to happen from time to time. "Because we can't schedule death," he explained.

What? I thought.

He went on to say that I would most likely need her assistance until I got up to speed, that she was always willing to help, and that I should just ask her when I needed assistance. I saw an expression cross her face that told me she would not be all that willing and hoped I'd never have to ask. I was told then that I should report to work the following Monday at eight in the morning, but he had one more question he needed to ask. Puzzled, I nodded. He asked, "Do you like coffee?"

I had never even tried coffee, so I answered, "No."

He replied, "You must learn over the next few days!" He turned and went into his office.

The girls had laughed at his statement, and I said, "He *was* joking, wasn't he?"

They explained that on Mondays and Fridays, the agents came into the office to spend the day and that they always brought coffee and doughnuts with them, and they told the new girls that they would never make a go of it at Southwest until they learned to drink coffee and must never refuse a doughnut! Needless to say, I did learn to drink coffee there, and to this day, to me, a doughnut is nothing with any other beverage but wonderful with coffee.

54

A Chance to Climb

Learning a new job can be quite overwhelming. At times, you come to believe that you will never be able to remember all those instructions, and then things suddenly start to fall into place. Mastering the terminology is a big part of learning a new job; sometimes, you feel the employees who were there before you are speaking a foreign language, but gradually that starts to click too. As I had suspected, I had very little assistance from the receptionist, but little by little, I just got it and then got it done. I felt I was doing a decent job, and I liked the job immensely. The agents had stopped teasing me and trying to convince me that black was white, and all in all, things seemed to be going well.

Not at the beginning, but after I had been at Southwest a couple of months, I noticed that our big boss (the president of the company) came out into the outer office and, taking a seat at an unoccupied desk in the rear of our space, seemed to be watching me. It made me nervous. This happened several times in the coming days, and then one day, he called me into his office, which confirmed my suspicions. Admitting that he had been observing me, he asked if I thought I was ready to move up the employment ladder. That scared me, for I was just beginning to reach a certain comfort level, one that I had almost despaired of ever reaching, and I was not sure that I wanted to start another struggle to learn. I asked him what he was offering, and he said supervisor of claims—at a substantial raise in salary.

We presently had a person in that position, and when I asked what was happening to her, he said she would no longer be working for the company. This was not the company's choice, for she was an excellent employee; she was quitting to stay at home to take care of an aging parent but that she would stay long enough to train me. I was flattered, but for me to make that decision would take some thought, and I told him that. I needed to talk to Brad, for he and I were also in the process of making some plans of our own that were still up in the air—namely, and I did not share this with my boss, that we planned to be married as soon as he was free, and as yet, that had not happened. And then we wanted to start our family.

Brad and I had talked a lot about our plans for the future, and even though Brad had three children already, we wanted children together. We knew that in these postwar years, pregnant women were only permitted to work a short period of time after becoming pregnant, and my husband-to-be had made it quite clear he preferred I not work *after* we had children, whether they were from our union or were his children, whose custody he intended to seek soon after we married.

Knowing this, did I want to let my boss, who was offering me this great opportunity so early in my working career, to go through all the time and expense to train me and put me in place and very possibly have to go through it all again in the near future when I would be giving it up to become wife and mother?

Without asking me to specify reasons for my request for time to make the decision, my boss asked if one week would be enough. He said that he was in sort of a rush, because the employee who was leaving needed to go as soon as it was possible and he wanted her to train me. I told him I would give him an answer in one week.

I was so proud that I had been chosen for this promotion, and I couldn't wait to get home to share it with my beloved, even though I knew it was very likely that I would not take it. That day was payday, and at lunchtime as I cashed my paycheck, I remembered thinking how much faster Brad and I would be able to get ahead with the much bigger salary I would make if I accepted the offered promotion. But was that what I wanted? Was that what Brad would want?

55

Spending Money

I realized that I, once again, was at a crossroads in life, not unlike when in high school I was offered and eventually turned down a worthwhile scholarship and going on for further education in exchange for what I knew in my heart of hearts was the only choice I could make. I had done it without looking back. Granted, it was a matter of the heart, and the current decision would be as well. It was the offered chance of being a wife to a wonderful man (I never had any reason to think he was anything but) and mother to his children. Would this be worth giving up this good job? Of course it would. Why would I even question it? I must trust what I know currently to be true and trust in God for the future.

As the afternoon wore on, I could barely wait for my workday to end so I could go home to tell my news and talk with my best friend and husband-to-be about the decision I felt I should make and get his stamp of approval. As it turned out, he met me at work and seemed to be in great spirits as if he also was bursting with news. Brad suggested I take the money I had earned that week and go shopping.

"Why don't you buy yourself a nice dress, and since winter will be here soon [it was Halloween, October 31, 1947], you should buy yourself a winter coat." He also told me, "On the way down to meet you, I saw a beautiful coat in the window of a department store, and it would look great on you. It's green and would go well with your hair. In fact, let's go there, and I'll buy it. That will leave you more money for other things you need."

56

Money Matters

Brad didn't seem to have much money. I knew that from his paycheck, money was sent to his mother, which she got to his children. He paid our apartment rent and had kept and paid rent for the apartment I had for myself for one month after I moved into his when he had released it back to our landlady. He had taken care of me when I was sick and up until I got a job. Then I started buying the groceries and my necessary clothes for work. Our apartment was furnished, so very few purchases were required there. He had purchased a small radio and a sewing machine for me on credit (he said that was to help build up his credit rating, for he may need it when we started to build our house and furnish it later). Other than that, we bought very little. He never gave me reason to doubt anything he did, but I sometimes wondered, since he had sold his businesses, where was that money? He had a small "sugar bowl" fund in which he placed a few bills each week, as he would say, "for a rainy day." He wasn't secretive about it and made sure I knew where it was, just in case—but just in case of what? Don't misunderstand me. Living with him, I saw and handled more money than I had ever in my life even seen, but I hadn't managed a household either. I didn't know the first thing about managing, and he patiently taught me.

Working exposed me to people with different lifestyles and life goals. Many spent money one day and hoped the next day would take care of itself. Planning to have money for down the road of life was a foreign concept to many; therefore, their philosophy seemed to be "We'll go to the movies today, the roller rink tomorrow, and if we don't have the money to buy a winter coat when it gets cold, we'll worry about that when we get cold!" These philosophies were all foreign to me, but I, like a child, am apt to want or do things others want or do and resent a little not being able to spend freely when I have money in my hand.

One day, as we started out for our usual walk, I said, "Let's go to the movies instead." He asked what I wanted to see. "Just anything," I said.

He was quiet for a few moments and asked, "Honey, aren't you happy with what we're doing? I'm trying to save a little so that, one day, we'll have something and can do anything we want, but right now, we can't afford to do much, and going to a movie just to be going is not high on my list as something to spend money for—money that we can't afford—in order to do it."

I wasn't accustomed to being denied anything from him, but I hadn't asked for much either, so I resentfully said, "What happened to all that money you got from selling your businesses?"

After a lengthy pause, Brad quietly said, "I bought some vacant farmland where we can build a house after we're married, and my mother is holding the rest for us to buy what we will need to build it. Do you want to spend that too?"

I felt so ashamed after I had cooled down. I really didn't want to go to a movie. I was just a little suspicious that he was trying to keep me from spending his money, or that he didn't want to spend any on me. After that, he was rather reserved for a few days. He probably thought I was just getting started to be the kind of high-maintenance wife about which lots of his friends complained, when in reality, I didn't really want to be "like the Joneses" any more than he did!

I came to highly appreciate my soul mate's great ability to handle money, to have what we needed and more besides. There were times when it was not easy, but he always seemed able to come through when it looked impossible. One of our sons recently said, "Dad had that Midas touch!" He did it honestly, and his goal for doing so always involved benefiting his family.

His family, from the beginning until the end, was the most important thing in his life. He was a country boy with little education, starting out with nothing. He said, "First, I desire to have a wife who loves me and being happily married, to have a big loving family, to be able to make a decent living, and to give my family a good life and to live a good Christian life myself as an example for them. That's all I ever wanted. Doing things like this involving my whole family together is just icing on the cake!" He had all that and so much more. I have quoted the foregoing from his answer to a question asked him by a newspaper reporter in Clermont County, Ohio, after a family water-skiing show on the Ohio River. The question asked of him was, "Did you start out in life planning to do this [family-oriented water-skiing shows]?" I never saw this question and his answer appear in the paper, but his answer to them that day meant so much to me that I jotted it down on a show program as I remembered it. It summed up his life goals.

57

Long-Awaited News

As we walked down the street toward the department store he had indicated, I noticed a familiar car parked in the employee lot of the insurance company where I worked; it looked remarkably like Brad's car, the one he had left with his brother in Kentucky. On further examination, I saw that it was! Now I was really puzzled.

At my questioning look, Brad nodded and said that he had found Daniel waiting for him when he got home from work and that he had brought Brad's car from Kentucky along with some very good news. A letter (which he dug out of his jacket pocket and handed to me) had come from Brad's local area county court in Kentucky, stating that Brad's "petition of release from an unsatisfactory marriage by Decree of Divorce" had been granted. That was all I needed to read. This was long-awaited and very good news!

We got into the car and sat there for, as it turned out, a long time as I told him the news that I had and what I thought I would do. All I needed was his stamp of approval.

With that, I went on to tell him why, in good conscience, I could not take the promotion, for I wanted what Brad did and that was to be a stay-at-home mother when we had children to care for. I could not take advantage of this opportunity, and later, when we had the children—his or one of our own— abandon the job and cause the company to have to once again look for another to fill this job. They had been too good to me. However, he told me I had to make that decision alone, that he would never want to have anything to say in a decision like that for me, for if I should later regret what I chose at his urging, I would resent his part in it and possibly blame him if it turned out wrong for me.

I had so wanted him to tell me what I should do, but he held firm. However, I could tell by his sweet smile that he approved of the decision I had told him was the only one I felt that I could possibly make. I learned as we went through our life together that when decisions arose that could have a dramatic effect and that concerned me personally, he would not involve himself in them. He also told me that the only way he would make my important personal decisions for me would be if I was totally and physically unable to make them myself.

When we finished our talk, I had made my decision, and as we pulled out of the parking lot, I was thinking, *How wise this man I will marry is proving to be.*

58

The Proposal

We arrived at the department store where Brad had seen the coat that he had described to me. There in its display window was the green coat, and I loved it on sight! It was forest-green wool trimmed in fake leopard fur. The fur trim started at the front neckline and went around the stand-up collar of the neckline, down the front, around the bottom of the coat, and up the front on the other side of the opening to the point of start, encircling the entire perimeter of the garment. The trim at the cuffs was from the same animal print.

Brad purchased the strikingly beautiful coat, and then we headed to the women's dress department. We selected several dresses and discarded all we had selected. The ones I tried did not fit; I still had not regained all of the weight I had lost while I was ill. What he had grudgingly approved and I had tried on hung on my thin frame like a sack. I didn't realize I had lost that much weight, but apparently I had.

Brad seemed to be searching for something for me that was special, something that would do the handsome coat justice, he said. I gave him the lead, for nothing I saw appealed to me after having tried them on. Finding nothing at the shop, we moved into another store and started the process all over again. This time, though, Brad seemed to feel he had found the one he'd like for me to have. It was a pearl-gray, fitted-top, dropped-waistline, long-sleeved soft cotton dress. It had a mock turtleneck collar with buttons down the back and a pleated skirt off the dropped waistline. I tried it on, and it fit. Gray is not a color I would have picked, but I liked it.

Then he bought me a pair of black medium-heeled leather pumps and nylon hose with seams, another first (nylon was just coming back after the war). Then he selected and bought me my first pair of jeans ... ever! Then came a navy-blue skirt, two basic pullover sweaters—one was pink. I protested here, for with my red hair, most pinks didn't work. He insisted it looked beautiful held close to my face. The second sweater, with long sleeves, was white. Then I chose and purchased several items of underwear. Brad left while I was choosing the latter and stated that he would be right back.

He came back with, of all things, a suitcase!

"And for what do we need that?" I asked.

"We need something to carry all we bought," he replied, and he shooed the clerk who had started to bag our purchases.

He hadn't bought a thing for himself. When I mentioned it, he said he had clothes at his mother's and didn't need any. With all our purchases folded neatly in the suitcase, except for the coat, which I wore, as it was turning cold, we returned to the car. When we settled in and got the heater running, I saw Brad look at his watch, so I asked him the time.

He said, "It's six fifteen. If I had thought about it, I could just have taken Daniel down myself."

Not until then did I remember Daniel. "Where is he?" I asked.

He answered, "I took him to the train station and sent him home. He said he had to be home early tomorrow. Now we're going to go home to get married! Oh, I guess I'd better ask. Will you marry me?"

See what a romantic my beloved was? I said yes, anyway. What I really said was, "Yes! Yes! Yes!"

59

A Dreaded Stopover

Halloween was crisp and cold under a full harvest moon. The drive to Denton was filled with excitement for me ... at least during the time I was awake. In the first place, it being the night for spooks and witches, we saw many signs of Halloween trickery pulled on many an unsuspecting rural homeowner, one he or she discovered when nature called in the middle of the night. Outhouses had been pushed over, and worse than that, some had been uprooted and placed in the middle of the main route of travel from Cincinnati southward on these mountainous roads.

On the trip to Denton, I barely could contain my excitement. The 250-plus-mile trip gave time (when I was awake) to do what we were very fond of doing—and that was to talk and share our dreams and ambitions (me, the dreams, and he, the ambitions). I have mentioned previously that when we talked, Brad's low-pitched voice with his Southern accent was so very calming. I could feel the slight vibration in his shoulder from his voice as I snuggled close. It was so soothing, and I was so tired from the day's work. All the excitement the day had brought was making me so drowsy, and I soon fell asleep.

I awakened, sensing the car had stopped. We had pulled off to the side of a street that at first looked unfamiliar to me. Upon further examining the landmarks, I realized we were in the same spot that we had stopped many, many times. It was the spot on Main Street in Denton, near the street where I had lived all my growing-up years, the spot where he had stopped to let me out when he brought me home from school.

My beloved greeted me with, "Good Morning." Looking around, I could see it was still nighttime.

I asked, "Why are we stopping?"

He told me that he thought we should go to our respective homes, one of the main reasons being to try to rebuild fences with my parents and to let them know our plans. His plan seemed wise, but no doubt, it was going to be hard for me. Also, he asked me to meet him in the same spot at nine o'clock the next morning, feeling that in the event my parents weren't ready to talk with him, we wouldn't push the issue by his making a possible unwelcome arrival at my parents' home.

It became apparent that Brad had made some advance preparations for our big day that was to take place the next day—November 1, 1947—knowing they would meet with my approval. He went on to tell me that we only had from the time he picked me up until about ten in the morning to manage all we had to do. We had to have an approved blood test with its accompanying document of proof, which was required before we could get our marriage license. After the blood test at a county-run health clinic in Denton to get our license, we then had to go to our county courthouse, a distance from Denton. This would have to be all done in order to be married by noon, for that was closing time for county offices on Saturdays. Just the mechanics of such an undertaking at best would be difficult to complete in the time we had allotted, but because Brad wanted to allow me time to talk to my parents after my father arrived home from work between seven and seven thirty, that left us little wiggle room, and I agreed to be there at nine o'clock or before.

Brad handed me the suitcase. At that moment, I realized the reason for the purchase for this seemingly unnecessary item!

As I started toward my home, the time was now near eleven o'clock at night. This meant that Papa would already be at work, and I was quite relieved. (My father's disapproval of me had a lot more impact than that of my mother; I don't know the reason for this, unless it was that his approval was harder to earn.) I arrived at the door of the house and saw just one light on in the house, my parents' bedroom. My mother promptly opened the door, pushed open the screen, and (never much on demonstrative action, she did not hug me) said, "Come on in. Glad you decided to come back. Better go on up and get to bed. It's late."

I guess it could have been worse; she could have locked me out!

60

Fear of the Morning

I found my usual spot in the bedroom for five girls, noticing my bed partner had changed. It was now to be my twelve-year-old sister, Shar. That pleased me. Shar awakened and with a little squeal gave me a quick hug and said, "I'm glad you're home!" I encouraged her to go back to sleep and tried to sleep myself. I don't think I slept much, for I dreaded the morning when I would have to face both my parents.

Early the next morning, I heard stirring that indicated my mother was up preparing for the day, and since I wanted to get a feel for what I was facing when Papa came home, I hurriedly dressed and went downstairs. Upon seeing me enter the room, Mama asked, "What made you finally decide to come home?"

I told her that with the situation with Brad, like it was with his marital status, I had been afraid to come. "Now that he is free to marry me, I wanted to come to..." *Be honest!* my conscience insisted. "It was Brad who thought I should come home and get your and Papa's blessing before we married," I told her.

"You want to marry him so that he will turn right around and do the same thing to you as he did to his first wife, is that it?" she responded.

"Mama, it's not like that at all. You just don't know him. After you meet him and talk to him, you will see what I mean! He's been your best ally in all that has happened," I pleaded to her.

"Talk's cheap, and we can't let that happen to you. You're not going anywhere; just wait until Papa gets home!" she exclaimed.

I didn't want to wait until Papa got home, but it didn't seem like I had a choice. Mama seemed dead set on keeping me from leaving; the front door of the house had been locked with a skeleton key, and I found the key had been removed from the door. That left only the back door, where Mama seemed to be keeping vigil to prevent me from leaving. I returned upstairs where my sisters were stirring, and they were so glad to see me. But fear for me seemed to be their greatest emotion. They began to express that they felt my parents would see that I did not leave the house even if they had to lock me up, as they had overheard Papa say. I feared this was already happening.

61

The Decision

My father came as scheduled, and I lagged behind when my sisters started downstairs.

I heard Papa grunt, "Well, where is she?"

In what seemed a long time afterward, Dee came upstairs and told me Papa wanted to talk to me. The time, I saw on the living room clock, was 8:20 a.m. No pleasure at seeing me showed on my dad's face. In fact, he was scowling darkly. I felt fear at what was coming as I sat down at his bidding to face him.

"Your mother says you have big plans for today. Well, it ain't gonna happen!" he growled. "The last thing your mother and I will allow is for you to marry that bird! You might as well get out of them city clothes and settle down and forget it. You ain't going anywhere!"

He had said his piece, and he settled back in his corner in his rocking chair with a scowl on his face that left no room for argument.

I looked into the adjoining room where I had seen my mother standing, listening just a moment before. I guess I was looking for some support from her. She was no longer in sight. I had such a sick, sinking feeling, and I guess, like a child seeks his mother when he is hurt, I sought mine, hoping she would fix things. She was nowhere in sight in that room or the kitchen. I turned around and spied my suitcase with my new coat draped across it in the corner, where I had left them, and thinking only to get away from the horrible situation I found myself in, I grabbed my belongings and ran through the open, unlocked back door and retraced the same route I had followed earlier that year back in May when I had left home after my fateful graduation-night scene.

191

I ran without pause until I was sure I was not being followed and that I was far enough away that I could get to Main Street and then double back to get to the point on the street where Brad was supposed to meet me. I saw a clock on the bank as I came out on Main Street and realized it was already a quarter to eleven, much too late to go on with our plans. I was later told by my sisters that Brad had driven by our house a number of times and my parents, noticing their nervous watching through the windows, made them take seats and stay away from the windows and to "let him worry all he wants to." Also, they told me that none of them knew I was gone for a while; they thought I was upstairs in the bedroom.

62

Joyful Reunion

I was a little better prepared this time than back in May. In reality, I had matured a lot. I had money and didn't depend on a taxi happening by; I went directly to a taxi stand and asked to be taken to Sunfish. I had decided going to where I knew I could eventually find Brad was the right choice, and that was where he was staying, at his mother's home. The taxi cost me three dollars this time. As mature as I thought I was, I didn't know about tipping, I suppose, and I paid him only three dollars.

Ma came out to meet me as she saw me get out of the taxi. She was rather flustered and told me Brad had been gone for a while. He had gone into town to meet me and wondered, "Did you all get your wires crossed?"

Shaking my head, I briefly told her the situation, and she asked if she could fix me something to eat. (It seems that we from the South always think food is the answer to all problems.) I told her I didn't want anything, for I was way too nervous to eat. She wondered why Brad hadn't returned after not being able to find me. I could only imagine how concerned he was when I didn't show, and I knew just forcing the issue with my parents would not have been his first action toward solving the problem. I too wondered if I had left Denton too soon. He may have still been waiting for me.

Suddenly, Ma said, "Here he comes. Get in the back room!"

I went to a bedroom that joined the kitchen, and she quickly grabbed my suitcase and shoved it in after me and closed the door. Almost immediately, she reopened the door and threw my coat onto the trunk beside the bed I was sitting on. This time she closed the door

193

only partially. I heard him come into the kitchen, and his mother asked him what had happened.

In a very worried and discouraged-sounding voice, he replied, "Mama, they must have her locked in; she didn't come, and I know she would have if she could! I drove by her house over and over, and I didn't see anyone, not even any of her sisters, and I knew I didn't have the right to just walk up and demand that they let her out! I don't know what to do."

I heard his mother quietly say in a very soothing voice, "We'll figure something out. First, go in the bedroom there and get me that bucket of apples; I need to start on them."

The door to the room I was in came open, and before he saw me, my beloved saw my coat. With a sharp intake of breath, he turned and saw me, and I went into his open arms. We just held each other for a while, for it was such a great relief for us to be back together safely and to be in each other's arms! I finally opened my eyes to see the smiling face of his mother watching us with tears in her eyes. That was when I realized both Brad and I were in tears as well.

63

Back in the Carrington Folds

It was much too late to continue with our wedding plans for that day, and the big problem was what to do with me for the night. For propriety's sake, there was no way that the bride- and groom-to-be could share the same quarters without being married, so the Carrington household set out to make it proper and find me accommodations. Brad's brother Daniel, who had come home then, was sent to get one of their sisters, Theresa, a favorite of Brad's, who lived in Denton and whom I had not yet met. I had met the three younger sisters; two of them, Treena and Nancy, I had met at his restaurant earlier in the year. The youngest one, Delores, was about twelve and lived at home. That left two brothers—Nolan, the youngest at fourteen, and an older one, Terrell, just a few years younger than Brad, who, after returning from the army, lived in Cincinnati.

When Theresa arrived, I immediately liked her. The best way to describe her is that she was the sweetest, gentlest person I had ever met (other than her brother, the one I planned to be with for life). Later, we were to realize, we were blessed with a daughter just like Theresa—our own sweet Kaylene.

Theresa solved our problem for us. She had an extra bedroom and would welcome having a guest for the next two nights, realizing that having missed our chances on Saturday, Monday was the soonest we could possibly be married.

Later that day, I once again had to leave Brad, though I had no doubts that we would be reunited. We spent the afternoon together. Brad was enjoying being reunited with his family, and I was enjoying being with him and getting to know the Carrington family. I learned they really knew how to lay a feast, and eating being one of my favorite activities, I was in hog heaven. (Later, after Brad and I were married, his mother spent a lot of time trying to fatten me up so I wouldn't look like a "picked jaybird"—her words!)

That day, I got to meet his father, who was spending time away from home and usual working place in a temporary placement, but he was home for the weekend.

Brad had prepared me for meeting his pa by saying, "My dad is a very quiet person, and he will probably say very little to you. Please don't feel he doesn't like you, as he may not talk to you at all. He is sometimes very shy around strangers, especially women."

How wrong he was! His pa, Paul Carrington, immediately slid over and placed a chair at the table beside himself, saying, "Sit down right here and make yourself at home. Pass Rachel the corn bread. Do you like home-churned butter? Here, have some of this."

Before that meal ended, he was sure I liked all his favorite foods, and in meals to follow, that was my place at his table, and he made sure he passed me *his* favorite dishes while declaring to me, "I am glad they are your favorite ones too!"

From that day on, I loved him dearly.

64

Wedding Bells Ring

November 3, 1947, our long-awaited wedding day, found me up early and anxiously awaiting Brad's arrival. I could not wait. I hadn't mentioned to anyone that I feared my father would suddenly appear and take me home, thus preventing our marriage from happening. We had learned over the weekend that Kentucky law prevented persons younger than eighteen from marrying without parental permission, and since I was only seventeen, I could possibly run into that restriction. Brad had learned that one of the three counties that made up the city of Denton might more strictly follow this rule than another. It was rumored that it was easier in one county to get around this provision. Since I was underage and no way were my parents going to give permission, we chose that county.

This turned out not to be the day that our chosen county was to be lenient, however, and they told us to return with my parents. However, the county clerk did give us some helpful information. He said he had heard on good authority that one of the other counties would bypass that rule if the couple had witnesses who would sign certain papers for the couple. We returned to Theresa's, and she and her husband, Bob, agreed to go as witnesses.

We were successful in the second county and were married by a justice of the peace. What joy! I was beginning to think it would never happen. We returned to Ma's and found that Brad had asked his brother to go and bring back his two older kids, and he had brought them to Ma's to celebrate with us. We took them for a ride in our car, which by then had been decorated in streamers; a few tin cans and old shoes were tied to the bumper. Later, we found the kids remembered that as their having gone to our wedding! We learned this at our fiftieth wedding anniversary when the kids were, metaphorically, toasting us and talking about many of their special memories. At that time, our sweet Kaylene said she had felt so special that she could go to our wedding and remembered that she thought her new mother was "the prettiest lady she had ever seen with long red hair, in a pretty dress, with the most beautiful green coat in the world!"

65

Postwedding Celebration

As was the custom in the hills of Kentucky, we had retired to our bed on our wedding night, when we were suddenly aware of a horrendous noise like metal pans being banged together and other very loud banging sounds accompanied by raucous laughter, whistling, and loud voices from the front of the house. (Luckily, Brad had clued me in to the fact that it would happen.) He had told me there would be more than just noise and that it was customary that the newlyweds be dragged out of bed—so being forewarned, we had gotten into bed fully dressed, and we didn't have to wait long before the mayhem had moved inside. A bunch of his friends and neighbors had gathered, and suddenly, we were looking up into the faces of several of them around our bed! This ceremony is known in the hills as a "chivaree."

The ceremony did not exclude the women of the community, for they were there to get in on the fun too. They had brought baked goods and snacks along with some drinks. It was not unusual to see some half-pint containers stuck in the back pockets of some of the men, and some quart jars of a clear liquid appeared as well. This custom also included procedures concocted to make consummation of the marriage vows, to put it daintily, a little uncomfortable! In this procedure, the groom had to ride a rail, usually a log carried between two men with a bit of bouncing going on, making the log a rough ride. The bride is bounced in a metal washtub. Even so, they treated me more gently than some I have seen since. (They were afraid they might hurt this little city girl!)

But hurt me they did ... but not from the bouncing. As they picked up the tub I was in, one of the handles caught my pinky finger between the handle and the tub. There was so much loud revelry going on, they did not hear my scream. I finally got their attention by pinching hard the arm of the man who was on the other side of the tub, pointing and motioning, thereby communicating the problem. Also at about the same time, shotguns were being fired into the air, and Brad was hit in the ear by a pellet from one of the shots. He suffered no permanent damage, but for a time, he could not hear out of that ear. We were the walking wounded as we crept back to our wedding bed later that night.

66

The Return to Ohio

The morning of November 4 dawned bright and sunny with a promise of the warmth that Indian summer often brings. We were in high spirits as we started home to Cincinnati. We had departed Brad's parents' home shortly after breakfast, promising to come back in a couple of weeks for Thanksgiving. It had been a great weekend, and I was so pleased with the big family that was now mine too! That brought to my thoughts the great difference between the family I had compared with the family Brad had and how his family had accepted me, though it was doubtful if my family would ever accept him.

Thinking of this, I said, "I am so sorry that things turned out the way they did with my family. If they could just realize how good you are to me!"

He replied, "I was thinking about your family too and wanted to ask you if you would consider just giving them another try. You need not be afraid they would try to keep you from leaving, for as your husband, I have a legal right to take you with me."

Since he had somewhat allayed my fears, I was eager to try again to make peace with my parents. When we arrived at their home in Denton, I went to the door alone, as we thought that to be the best method.

My father was sitting in his corner in the living room, smoking as usual. I caught a glimpse of my mother quickly leaving the room as I walked to the door. My dad invited me to come in when I knocked on the screen door (the inner door was open). I told him that I was married now, since the day before, and that we were on our way back to Cincinnati, where we had an apartment and jobs. But I told him I hadn't wanted to go back without my giving him and Mama a chance to meet and get to know my husband. Papa had never met him. He continued sitting, making absolutely no indication he was hearing me, as his frozen, unsmiling face did not change.

I started to get somewhat angry, for I had made all the effort I knew to make, with no response from him, and I said, "Okay, if that's the way you want it, that's the way it'll be. If you don't want to accept my husband—one of the nicest, kindest men you'll ever meet; one who has taken such great care of me and has been so seriously empathetic to you and Mama concerning your worrying about me leaving home like I did—then you can forget about me too, for I won't be back."

With that, I opened the door and started to leave. I hadn't gotten completely through the door when he said his first words. "Well, when am I going to meet this husband of yours?"

"Right now if you want to," I answered.

With that, I went to the car and said, "He says he wants to meet you!"

Brad followed me into the house, and immediately, my dad stood and extended his hand. Brad shook it and said, "Brad Carrington. It's nice to meet you."

Brad and my dad talked for a while about such things as their jobs. Papa was pleased to find that Brad also had a railroad job. Before Brad left, my dad was treating him as if he was a well-liked acquaintance. I was so glad Papa had welcomed him, and it seemed that Papa liked him from that day forward. Mama didn't meet him (she had seen him back in the early spring but was not aware of his identity) until several weeks later on Thanksgiving when we stopped for a turkey leftover snack with them before heading back to Cincinnati. That was our second visit to Denton as a married couple. On that visit, my mother fell under the charms of my handsome husband, and that special relationship lasted until my mother's death in 1989.

67

The Tardiness

On Tuesday after our wedding day and our short visit with my dad in Denton, we were headed back to Cincinnati, and I suddenly remembered our jobs! We had both left Cincinnati meaning to return to our jobs on Monday. It was Tuesday, and we wouldn't be back on the job until Wednesday, having missed two days. I supposed calling in to report our absences back then as now would have been the proper way to handle this situation. We both hadn't, and honestly, my job had never entered my mind. As it was, we would just have to take our chances that they would take us back.

On Wednesday morning, I went into my workplace early, for I knew my boss was always in early. I found him sitting in the coffee room with a cup of coffee working on a file. He looked up as I came in and said, "So you decided to grace us with a visit, huh?"

He will fire me for sure, I thought. I started with, "I got married Monday, but the wedding was supposed to be Saturday." I told him the whole story, even admitting that I hadn't even thought of the job until just before we headed back to Cincinnati.

He seemed to sit and consider what I had told him for a little longer than I expected, and I hoped it didn't mean he was not approving my absence and that I no longer had a job. Then he started to laugh of all things! He said that was the first time ever he had gotten that excuse from an employee who was late to work. Puzzled, I said to him, "I'm not late. I wasn't at work Monday and Tuesday, and I didn't notify anyone not to expect me. I don't know if being absent to get married is excusable, but I suspect if an employee doesn't notify an employer of a planned absence of any kind by or at least on the day of the absence in emergency situations, the absence is inexcusable."

"You are correct in the abstract you presented, but here's the way I see it. Our policy here is to give newlyweds two days' salary as a wedding present, and if the wedding is on a workday and the employee is absent for the two days, he is not docked for the time, because that is the amount he would be getting as a wedding gift, and the absence is not tallied. In your case, you were off two days and your reason was your wedding, hence two days' pay and no absence; however, because you were tardy in reporting your wedding, that's going down as a tardy—an excused tardy—because the reason, being off to be married, is a legitimate excuse for not being present. Now get out of here before I change my mind. By the way, Rachel Periwinkle, the next time you get married, tell somebody … before the wedding!"

Oh, how did he remember my horrid middle name … I didn't even want to remember it myself! However, the twinkle in his eye was all I needed to put my mind at ease. I wanted to reply to the "next time" part of his warning with, "It isn't ever going to happen!"

68

The Promotion

I waited until the end of the week my boss had given me to give him my decision about the promotion he had offered earlier. When I had explained the reason for my turning it down, he indicated that even though he was disappointed I wouldn't be taking the job, he understood and appreciated my reason for turning it down.

He went on to tell me that a number of years before, his own wife had been offered a promotion in the job she held at the time. For the same reasons, she had turned it down, and putting her family first, she had not worked for over twenty years. Finally, she rejoined the workforce. Then she could dedicate the necessary time and effort to the job without splitting her time and attention between job and family. He indicated that he felt that their children had benefited from this. Then, when she decided she was ready to work, she took some refresher courses and kept involved in current events and trends, so working again did not require a major adjustment.

"But in the meantime, how much longer will you stay?" he asked. I told him I probably would stay at least through the winter, because we were moving back to Kentucky and planned to build a house, and we would wait for warmer weather to start the process. He agreed that two weeks' notice would be ample time to announce my leaving.

No one in our office was offered the promotion I turned down; it was filled by an older experienced worker from another insurance company.

69

Future Uncertainty

When Brad had first come to Cincinnati, he had taken a job with a railroad as a freight handler. It was not the type of job he wanted to stay in all his working years, but at the time, it was paying the bills.

His dream was to find work in Kentucky and to raise his kids there, but there still wasn't much work available in those parts. Consequently, what happened in the next couple of years would direct what we would have to do. At that time, finding employment in Kentucky was looking more and more promising. Rumors were rampant that several coal companies were laying the groundwork for moving their operations into the foothills of the area surrounding Denton, and the economy was slowly improving. Brad's brother Daniel was urging us to come home to Kentucky, and Brad was seriously considering it but still held back from giving up his job.

Knowing how Brad thought and planned, I knew he would be certain employment opportunities were there before he pulled up stakes in Ohio and moved to Kentucky. Then he would work on convincing me, and that would take very little effort. That was the way my beloved worked—he knew how afraid I was of change. Because of my reluctance of stepping out into the future fearlessly, he paved the way by checking all the angles and encouraging me to take these really scary plunges hand in hand with him. He never let me down.

Until then, he stayed with the railroad. After returning from the absence for our extended wedding weekend, his reason for missing work was accepted but not with the surprise bonuses of my approved "tardiness."

70

Thanksgiving Number One

A few weeks after our wedding, Brad and I returned to Denton for Thanksgiving. I was looking forward to seeing his family again and to take my new husband to Mama and Papa's so he could meet the rest of my sisters and brothers. We were to go there for turkey leftovers the day after Thanksgiving. Mama had written a letter asking us to come for Thanksgiving, but since we had already made plans to go to Brad's home, I suggested that we come the next day for leftovers. Mama graciously agreed and seemed very pleased for us to come the following day.

We left right after work on Wednesday evening to go to Kentucky for the holiday. When we arrived at Brad's mother's home, everyone was in bed, which we expected since it was pretty late. Entering the house through the kitchen, the residual aromas of the evening meal served quickly to remind us that we had not eaten since our noon meal.

Brad winked at me and said, "Want me to fix you my very favorite dish, the one I missed so much when I was in the navy?"

Thinking a meal like that would take too long to prepare, I said, "Maybe some other time."

He said, "I'm going to fix me one; might as well make it two." "Oh, okay. Go ahead," I agreed.

In just a few minutes, Brad returned with a large serving bowl filled with a lumpy-looking liquid and two spoons. On closer examination, I recognized the bowl's contents—corn bread and milk! I loved corn bread and milk! We made short order of the delicious concoction. I could see he was pleased that I liked one of his favorite snacks, and eating it together out of the same bowl made it extra special.

Our Thanksgiving with Brad's family was wonderful. So far, his whole family seemed to have accepted me into the Carrington family with love. Brad's grandmother Maggie Kennedy Minton was there, and I could see where Brad's mother, Alene, came by her frank, to-the-point way of speaking. His grandmother had set the mold. She told it like it was.

This was even more evident later in our marriage after we began our family together. The incident I remember that hurt and embarrassed me was a remark his grandmother had made to no one in particular but to the gathering in general. Brad and I had just come through the door at Ma's house with our six-week-old Margene. Grandma Minton had not seen me since the baby was born, but she had been told I wasn't breast-feeding my baby. Highly disapproving this choice even though she knew the reason was that I did not have adequate milk for the baby, she remarked, "You can't tell me she doesn't have enough milk with tits that big!" I am certain my red face plainly showed my extreme embarrassment; in fact, I was so embarrassed I wanted to leave.

Brad put his arm around me and pulled me close and said, "She says just what she thinks; don't let that bother you. She doesn't mean to hurt you!"

Even though she scared me, I did feel she always approved of me.

The food Ma prepared was delicious and plentiful. She had the usual Thanksgiving turkey and trimmings as I was accustomed to while growing up. She didn't have the chestnut dressing Mama always prepared, but both her and Ma's dressing was a sage corn bread type—Ma's minus the chestnuts. Mama's presentation of her holiday meals were just a little fancier than Ma's. Ma's was just plain farm country with a variety of vegetables, a bigger variety than Mama offered. Mama prepared cold potato salad; Ma's was of the hot variety. Ma had a variety of pies and cakes; Mama had cakes, and one of her regulars for Thanksgiving was a homemade fruitcake that she made each year. Ma had a molasses stack cake. Mama saved this special cake for the Christmas dinner. (It was made just before Thanksgiving and aged until Christmas and was a favorite of all. If he could get by without Mama catching him, Papa would lace it with rum while it aged!)

It would be extremely hard to determine which dinner was better; both Ma and Mama were excellent cooks!

As it turned out, Brad and I got to have two full, delicious Thanksgiving dinners the first year of our marriage; Ma served her dinner at noon, and Mama's was at about four thirty, both on Thanksgiving Day! No leftovers for us; both were the family meal for the Thanksgiving season. We were glad that we did not have to return to Cincinnati that evening. It would have been an uncomfortable drive on such full stomachs.

71

First Winter

The winter of 1947/48 was a wonderful experience for Brad and me. It was our first winter as husband and wife. Even though we had been together since July, we seemed to experience new things constantly and savor everything new that we did together. We went roller-skating several times that winter, and Brad taught me how to do more than just move forward ... once I got over my fear of falling. To learn how to do skate routines, I was to learn that some falling must take place and that the floor comes up fast and hard. Brad finally had a skating partner—not as good as he was accustomed to with some of the young girls with whom he skated at Frankfort, but he seemed happy with me. When we went out and weren't skating or walking (we walked less than normal, for it was very cold that winter), we did go to an occasional movie. We saw Gone with the Wind, White Christmas, and other movies whose names I don't recall. We did not have television, which was the pastime that most people seemed to enjoy in the drab months of cold. Television sets were just starting to appear in stores, but few had them in their homes. We still preferred sitting or walking (weather permitting) and talking more than any other activity we could do, and on weekends and in the evenings after work, we spent many hours doing just that.

Our first Christmas together was a memorable one. We did not decorate for Christmas, as we were going to Kentucky to spend Christmas with our families. We did not know if we would be able to see Brad's children. Ma had written us and told us she would see if they could spend some time with us, but when the time came, it didn't happen. We had gifts for them, and so did Ma. Early evening on Christmas, Brad delivered the gifts and did get to briefly see his kids. That evening when he returned, he again stated to me, "I will someday soon have my kids with me, and we can plan on it happening! I don't want to do anything until I can have a home for them, and an apartment in Cincinnati is not the way to go. The home I will build will be their home, and as soon as I can get work down here, we will be coming back to Kentucky."

Again for the Christmas holiday dinners, we were able to spend time with both our families. I was so happy to see how Mama and Papa welcomed Brad into our family. My sisters loved him already; I don't know about my brother Chandler, for he wasn't around us much while we visited. My brother Jason, my youngest brother, was a fun-loving child and was always saying funny things. Brad liked him right off. Brad made a hit with the younger sisters Ali and Patrece by playing with them. As far as I knew, the family had completely accepted him.

Being with the Carrington family was a treat for me. They were open and caring toward me and I was becoming very close to them. They had welcomed me with open arms, especially Brad's sisters, Nan and Treena. I believe it to be because their ages were close to mine, both just a little younger than me. Nan and Treena were planning to leave home to find work but needed to live with relatives for a short while—at least until they had saved a little money. They sought Brad's approval to live with us, if they came to Cincinnati to find jobs.

Brad's brother Terrell lived in Cincinnati with his wife and two infant daughters. Because he expected to stay in Cincinnati, he had offered his sisters a place to stay with his family. He had returned to a good job after his stint in the US Army, and that job held promise for his future. When Brad learned his sisters wanted to stay with us, he encouraged them to go to Terrell's instead, as we probably would not be staying in Cincinnati. As soon as any work came to the Denton area he wanted to be there to find a job and to build our house in Sunfish. All indications were that this would start to happen soon. The girls made the decision to live with Terrell and his family while job hunting in Cincinnati.

Terrell's job with H. H. Myers, a meat processing and packing plant in Cincinnati, was different from a lot of manufacturing jobs to which the military were returning. Many factories were directly connected with the manufacturing of parts and supplies for the war effort, and those companies needed time for retrofitting for peacetime manufacturing, and they were not immediately ready to take back employees.

The factories were also facing the task of retaining the added wartime employees in positions as much as possible to avoid large layoffs. Then there was the rehiring of returning military. Many women had taken jobs in factories where women had not worked prior to the war, and all this meant more people needing placement and fewer positions to be filled. On top of all this, demand for manufactured products had dropped off. This all combined to require a longer time to make the changes for businesses in order to return to regular operation. Normal attrition took care of some of the returning-employee placement problems, but the military returnees first needed placement in positions comparable to those left upon their call to wartime duty before new hiring could be done. I imagine that because some of the discharged military were using their "rocking chair" money before returning to their jobs, it helped in the task of finding space for those ready to return.

Brad did return to his job in the Newark navy shipyards in New Jersey within the time allotted to his return, but only after he realized that he had no marriage to return to and no real reason to want to stay in Kentucky. As it turned out, he only stayed there about six weeks. He missed his family, and his desire to be closer to his kids increased. He left that job to start a business in Kentucky.

72

Good News Just Keeps Coming

In February 1948, a letter from Daniel came to us in Cincinnati. In this letter, Brad learned that a large coal company had moved operations into the mountains surrounding the Denton, Sunfish, and Rolling Rock areas and were to begin a strip-mining operation, and all of these were close to Brad's mother's home. In this letter, Daniel told Brad that they needed heavy-equipment operators. Brad, who spent several years in the prewar Civilian Conservation Corps (commonly referred to simply as the 3Cs or CCs), had training on this type of equipment. Daniel had picked up the training, too, through his military service, and he had already gotten a job with this coal company as a shovel operator and was soon to start work. This was a great opportunity for Brad. He and I immediately gave leave notice to our employers, and by the first of March, we were ready to move to Kentucky.

Toward the end of February, I had begun to have some unusual problems and was afraid whatever illness I had had the previous summer was coming back. I was very tired and found it hard to stay awake at work, even though I was sleeping well at night. I started being nauseous, and I had not been nauseous during my summer illness. Brad made an appointment for me to see a doctor the landlady had recommended. On the walk to see the doctor, I became faint and actually lost consciousness. If Brad hadn't been there to catch me, I would have fallen.

After a bit, however, I was able to finish my walk to my doctor's appointment. After examining me thoroughly, the doctor told me to get dressed and come into her office. In her office, she began to go over with me all that she had learned by the examination and the tests she had run. She said, "Mrs. Carrington, you aren't ill; you're pregnant! All symptoms you have mentioned are symptoms that can indicate pregnancy. Some of them should go away shortly, some will last longer, and some, such as your drowsiness, will cause you to need a lot more sleep, and that will stay with you throughout your term and even after you have given birth, for a time. As far as the fainting, even though it happens on rare occasions, you may never experience it again. You were probably anxious about coming here today. It often is anxiety during pregnancy that triggers it."

73

Busy Times

Because there was so much demanding Brad's attention when we returned to Kentucky, we postponed building our house that spring and summer. The startup of strip-mining had gotten off with a bang. Sunfish's once-quiet roads were teeming with truck traffic hauling coal, equipment, and workers. Brad immediately was hired to run what he called a "drag line," and part of that time, he ran a Caterpillar bulldozer. He saw the opportunity to make additional money by buying and selling coal from the company for which he built roads and stripped coal.

That required buying a truck, which he did, taking some of the money he had set aside for building our home. After work, he would go back to the stripping site and haul loads of coal to private homes. People in these rural areas used coal almost exclusively as the only source of fuel for cooking, water heating, and heating of their homes, and with it being so necessary, the market was good for these local haulers, keeping Brad very busy. We had very little leisure time together, and I missed that, but I knew it was necessary.

74

Settling into Country Living

That summer's activities were quite a learning experience for me, and my new mother-in-law was my teacher. She excelled in all the duties of a homemaker, and I was an avid student. I loved to please my husband, and what better way, in my mind, was there than to do things the way his mother did them! She always had a large garden, and most of what we ate that summer came from her garden and our meat from the farm. From these sources came our meals after the growing season ended as well. Pork was the meat of choice, mainly because it could be cured and kept over long periods of time, and with no freezers and very few refrigerators commonly being used by the rural homes in those days, types of preservation of food besides refrigeration were essential.

Brad's dad and his brother Daniel, who lived at home, always kept the season's supply of pork plentiful. Hog killing was a neighborhood project where farmers helped other farmers during the slaughter season, which commonly came after the first killing frost. It was a time when it was cold enough to keep the fresh meat from spoiling while the curing process of parts of the animal and canning of other cuts were taking place.

When summer finally arrived, the growing season brought on work with which I was familiar—the canning of fruits and vegetables, for I had helped my mother prepare the foods she canned, but I had little experience with the growing of them. At my family's home, we bought what we had from peddlers from nearby farms and truck patches. Prior to marriage, my job was helping with the washing and peeling to prepare the fruits and vegetables for canning—not the actual preserving of the food. I had no knowledge of this phase of the operation ... but I did learn, and Ma was a patient teacher.

I worked with Ma in all her food-preservation activities that summer. I learned to can a large variety of vegetables and fruits. Fruits not grown in her garden or orchard, such as a variety of berries, were picked from uncultivated fields and wooded areas and made into canned stewed fruits or jams, jellies, marmalades, and preserves. I also learned processes for canning meats, as freezers were virtually unheard of in those parts. I felt I could never come up to the excellence level of my husband's mother, but I was intent on being the best I could be. I later learned from overhearing a conversation between Brad's mother and one of his sisters that Ma was very pleased with my progress. She was telling my sister-in-law that she had taught me to make jelly but that my jelly had turned out far better than her own! Her approval was so very important to me.

75

The News Brings Change

Later in that summer, Brad told me he had found a place we could rent; actually, it was in the process of being built and would be ready shortly before our baby was due in early November. He also told me that he planned to go to a lawyer to start custody hearing procedures in order to gain custody of his three children. He knew how much I was looking forward to having our family all together.

He contracted the rental house and went to see his lawyer to file the custody suit. The house was planned to be ready for us in early October, but he had found that the custody had to wait for the spring circuit court. Also, my husband had contracted to have our own house built and for it to be started in early spring the following year. Brad was finally bringing in enough money to be able to replenish that which he had taken from our building funds in order to buy his truck and had been able to put away extra money that would be needed when our family grew larger as it was soon to do. This was all really exciting for both Brad and me; we could now get on with our lives as we had planned.

76

Well Worth the Wait

As my pregnancy progressed, it didn't take much to make me extremely tired. Ma and I were using the last of the garden produce—in this case, tomatoes, which she had meant to peel and put away whole into canning jars, which was a simple, easy way to process them. She was doing this batch for us to take with us when we moved into our rented house. I remembered that, on the few occasions we had eaten out, Brad would order tomato juice (instead of a soda) to drink with a meal. And because of that, I knew he liked juice. Since I was actually doing the processing under her guidance, I asked if I could do juice. Of course, it was fine with her, but because she knew I was tired, she explained it was more difficult to make juice and would take longer, but if I wanted to do it, she would show me how. I did the juice.

After I finished the juice and washed up the canning utensils, Ma suggested I go lie down for a while, for she could see I was very tired. I agreed to do that and went into the adjoining room to rest.

Soon afterward, Brad came home from work, and noticing the juice-filled canning jars that his mother had pointed out were ours to take home, he asked, "Why juice? I really like tomatoes."

His mother said to him, "Young man, don't you dare say that to Rachel! She has worked really hard to make juice for you. She thought juice is what you wanted, so accept it and be happy with it."

That was maybe the first of many times I was aware that she stood up for me. She was not demonstrative, and she did not express how she felt about the ones she loved, but it showed in many ways. She became a much-loved second mother to me.

I didn't have a hard pregnancy or long labor with my first child. The hardest part was the extreme heat of the long summer, but the discomfort was all forgotten when I first saw the baby. My first glimpse of our little new Carrington was of a freshly scrubbed little face swaddled all in pink and in her daddy's arms. Our little Halloween pumpkin was born October 31, 1948, exactly one year from the day we made the drive to Kentucky to be married. Because I had some postdelivery problems that kept me in the hospital five days—longer than most stays—I missed my baby shower that my sisters had planned for me on November 3. (Little Margene was not expected until November 5.) The birth of our first child was such a blessed event, and Brad and I were so thankful for this precious addition to our family.

77

Mixed Signals and New Babies

My relationship with Mama remained strained during the first year of my marriage and would sometimes revert to the strained feeling, even after my babies started to come along. I don't know what bothered her, but I suspected it was because of my good relationship with my brothers and sisters. She actually seemed jealous that they cared for me. Case in point: they were often begging her to let them stay overnight at my home, and the way she reacted to their requests in her remarks made me feel that it was jealousy.

I needed my mother then and would often call on her for advice concerning my babies or myself during my pregnancies. Oftentimes, it was just to be with her. She was ready and willing to help me during those times, and our relationship seemed once again to be improving. It was with the birth and afterward of my firstborn, Margene, that I noticed the first tenderness for me from Mama that I ever remember.

I realize that I am painting a bad picture of my mother in these statements, and I really hate that, but I need to tell this. I do realize that my mother always had a lot on her plate when she was raising her family, and she did a remarkable job with what she had to work. A lot of that time, she had to do it alone, for Papa went through periods of heavy drinking with lost income, which had to make her struggles even harder. She always seemed to be tense, impatient, and angry, and as a child, I felt she was unapproachable. Consequently, I did not bring my questions or problems to her. Children often get the wrong opinion of parents—or at least different opinions than others in the same family do. Dee did not feel this way at all.

Mama never spoke of problems between us. The only way I can describe her actions is that, as I mentioned before, she seemed jealous. I had hard feelings for a while, though, concerning my graduation night. Brad was putting forth a lot of effort in encouraging me to me get over it, and I gradually did put the hard feelings aside.

For me, since I, as yet, did not drive, taking the bus into town was the only way to go to doctors' appointments, and the bus only ran once a day, going into town early morning and returning from Denton at five in the evening each day. On a few occasions, I missed the return bus. As I mentioned earlier, Papa never had a car, so he could not help me. On those days, my parents welcomed me when I showed up at their door, and Papa would try to find a ride home for me. On other days, they offered me a place to stay and rest and get a bite to eat between bus rides. As I indicated earlier, my husband had won them over, and their approval of my marriage seemed very high. During those visits with them, my mother was very pleasant and treated me wonderfully. The unpleasant encounters with her had always come when my brothers and sisters were present. I was getting mixed signals. I just didn't understand her yo-yo behavior.

My mother visited with me during the five days I had to spend in the hospital after Margene was born, and I tremendously enjoyed her visits. During one of those visits, she told me that my daughter was to have an aunt that would be younger than her. Mama assumed that the baby she was expecting would be a girl, since eight of the ten children she already had were girls. And as she suspected, little more than four months after my own child was born, my little sister Lucy, my children's aunt, was born on March 5, 1949.

My baby sister was Papa's pride and joy. I saw how much he enjoyed that little blonde, high-energy girl. Yes, she was spoiled, but she knew she was loved, and her confidence was through the roof. Her active, imaginative energy got her into a lot of trouble and gave Mama fits, especially after Papa passed away. He died when Lucy was six years old.

78

Moving and a Hint of the Future

At the end of November 1948, our rental house was ready for our move in. We had no furniture, except for my sewing machine and Brad's small radio, as our apartment in Cincinnati had been furnished. After that, we were living with Ma, so we had to buy furniture. Again, in order to further fortify creditworthiness, we bought the furniture on an installment plan and bought only what was necessary to furnish the little two-bedroom house we were renting. I had wanted to buy a baby bed first thing; the egg basket I was using as a bed for Margene was soon going to be too small. I had seen cribs in a Sears Roebuck catalog that looked nice but seemed rather expensive. I mentioned that to Brad's sister Theresa, asking her advice on the purchase, and she said she had a bed she would give me. After seeing the crib, it was just what I wanted.

Just shortly before Brad and I met, Theresa had lost a little boy, Michael, to a very serious illness. The crib she had given me was an attractively styled maple wood with mattress and linens that she had used for Michael. I suppose she and her husband didn't expect to have more children and actually didn't for quite a while afterward.

The needed furniture and appliances were delivered to our new rental house, and after we purchased a coal-burning heating stove and Brad had delivered the necessary coal, we moved into the house. By that time, it was close to Christmas, and we already had snow on the ground, making moving more difficult.

The first weekend we lived in our new house, Brad was able to get his children for a few days. This was the first time I had kept the little boy Barry overnight, and he cried for his grandma (apparently, he spent a lot of time with his maternal grandmother). Finally, when I got the two babies quieted down, I was able to go to bed.

Whew! On this rare weekend with two babies and two other young children, it was good practice for when we would have a bigger family.

Back in those days, a wife and mother had the near total responsibility of taking care of the children, and today, when I see my sons-in-law and grandsons feeding, diapering, and bathing their babies, my first thought is, *Why didn't Brad help me that way?*

It is then that I remember. He didn't have time! Where the modern menfolk work eight hours and come home, there is time left in the day. In Brad's earlier working life, eight hours was not even half of the day he put in. When that was finished, he rushed home, grabbed a bite to eat (which I had to have ready) so he could get on to a second job and then, possibly, go on to a third. He had to do that to get ahead or, at times, just to break even.

79

A Heartwarming Early Surprise

In April, Brad's attorney notified him that he had filed the suit for custody of his three children and that the courts should be sending out written notifications to him and his ex-wife in a few weeks. As I stated before, it was and still is very difficult for a father to be awarded full custody of minor children in the state of Kentucky, and in most cases where men win the custody, it is because the mother has been declared an unfit mother. Brad did not have a vindictive nature, and even though he could have rightfully filed his suit with a stronger reason, he had filed with one less harsh and witnesses to sustain it, one that his lawyer thought could suffice. Consequently, because of his confidence of winning the case, his attorney warned him we should be prepared for a substantial change in the size of our family.

Early in June, Daniel came to Brad to tell him that his ex-wife would like to meet with Brad, his lawyer, and Daniel (Daniel was a witness in the custody suit), and she had asked them to come to her home. Daniel told him the meeting had to do with the custody hearing. They went to her house and found her there with her lawyer, along with her mother and one of her sisters. Her attorney started the informal meeting with the reading of a prepared legal document that he had brought to the meeting. The document stated, in essence, that his client, in order to avoid public embarrassment or harm to her character, was willing to settle the matter out of court if the parties could agree to a revised proposal that was to be presented. She was willing to give up the custody of the three children to their natural father for certain considerations ... and he listed the following: if plaintiff would agree to make payment of a specified dollar amount, which the defendant needed to pay off an outstanding debt she owed to a local grocery store; an agreement from the plaintiff and his attorney to refrain from making public certain damaging statements made as a part of the suit against her; and an agreement by the plaintiff to defendant's visitation rights with their three minor children at times and frequency to be determined later between the two of them.

At a nod from his attorney, Brad was more than ready to sign this agreement to pay the requested amount and, hopefully, take the children home that day. As it turned out, not only did they have the kids ready to send home with Brad, they had their meager supply of clothing ready as well. None of the dresses I had made for Kaylene, the sweaters we had bought for the children, or the overalls and shoes we had purchased for little Brad were in the bag.

At first I was angry, but Brad quickly smoothed my ruffled feathers by saying quietly, "Just look at what we have gained," indicating the three little ones.

Immediately, I was very ashamed at my outburst. That certainly was okay. I could make more dresses, and overalls were something the little guy didn't like, anyway. We could buy him some jeans. And shoes! We were to learn that Brad Jr. could go through a pair of shoes a month. We hadn't bought anything for the baby, Barry, for he had visited only once before.

80

Preparing to Help

Never in my wildest dreams would I have ever guessed that when Brad returned from the meeting with his ex-wife that the size of our family would have exactly doubled. I went from having a family of one child to having four children. I was eighteen years old, had a baby daughter of six months, a two-year-old toddler son, a five-year-old son, and an eight-year-old daughter. To make it even more interesting, approximately nine months later, I was to have a new little daughter, making our fifth child, and I was still under twenty years old. Little did I know then that, eventually, our family would consist of mother, father, and seven children by the time I celebrated my twenty-third birthday!

During this period of our lives, Brad was working close to twenty hours per day, and I missed him. Mostly I missed our long talks, but there was no time. Our house was in the process of being built, and when we had run out of the money that Brad had set aside for the house, we managed to pay as we built due to Brad's long hours of working.

I had begun to realize that I needed to be more responsible for so much of what Brad had been doing in the past ... for instance, all the driving into town for groceries and supplies, going to the doctor, and all the activities that created need for transportation to go into Denton (the closest town to our area). I knew I needed to take some of the responsibility off my husband, and to do this, I must learn to drive. I mentioned this to my beloved husband, and he agreed. Riding the bus was not an option anymore, for I could not leave the children home. Going to town on the bus took all day, and carrying groceries on the bus was out of the question. More mouths to feed meant more groceries to buy (and carry).

I had found a little church about a mile from where we were building our home, and it was difficult and dangerous to walk the distance with four children on a busy highway with no sidewalks. Brad could not help in this, for he worked weekends as well. In fact, he had begun to haul coal four hours each day and all day on the weekends for the company he worked for daily as a dozer operator, and at thirty dollars per load, we finally felt we might catch up. In this day and time, this seemed like, and was, good money—especially to a man who knew what it was like to work all day, daylight to dark, for one dollar per day, clearing new ground (land that had never been cultivated) with saw, mattock, shovel, and scythe!

By that time, our 1941-model Plymouth (the one bought used that had served him well in his taxi business and then was used as our family car), four hundred thousand miles and two motors later, had given out, and we needed a car. New cars were still hard to find in these postwar years, so Brad set out to find me a good used car and to teach me to drive. He found me a nice, clean car, a 1937 Packard that had been driven by an older couple and had low mileage. It was just what we needed for our family. After I had learned to drive, I could then take on more of the necessary errands on my own.

My little family really enjoyed our church. I don't believe the children had ever been in Sunday school, and it was something to which they looked forward each week. I hadn't been going to that church but a few weeks when I was asked to teach the junior class. This was a class of children from nine to thirteen years of age. I loved teaching that age group, for they seem so eager to learn, and that is the group I have taught throughout my Sunday school teaching years. One of my favorite activities with my students then, especially in vacation Bible school, was the Bible sword drill. In my own experience from my childhood Sunday school years, this drill taught me how to quickly locate the books and learn the format of the Bible. Because of this, today, I can more quickly follow scripture references given by ministers as the basis of their sermons. For this, I thank God for all the good Christian leaders I had growing up, and I hope my own students also benefited through me.

81

Difficulties and Rewards

In late October, when the weather started to be cold with frequent rain, all outside work on our house—then under construction—had to be curtailed for the winter. The house was completely under roof with all the doors and windows installed. One side of the house had all floors, room partitions, and part of the drywall in place. We moved into the almost-finished side while Brad was trying to get the rest of the drywall in on the side of the house where the floors had been laid. Our builder was contracted to do the outside of the house, and he had finished what he was supposed to do. With Brad's little time to be home, I could see no way that he would find time to work on the house. I encouraged him to have the builder do the inside work as well as the outside.

He replied simply, "I don't have the money to hire him."

We actually moved into the house with the side nearest completion only partially finished. By then, my second pregnancy was most obvious and was beginning to be more difficult, not the easy time I had experienced with little Margene.

During that fall and winter, Brad did take some time off from his second job of coal hauling, partly because the roads to the strip mine were so bad due to the heavy rains and partly because he badly wanted to get the house livable before extreme cold set in. As it turned out, he didn't get all the drywall in place, and it was a struggle to keep out the cold.

I was worried that the two boys would have problems that winter, for they were prone to a physical affliction called croup—or so I had been prewarned by their mother and my mother-in-law, who were concerned about their living in a house that could not keep out the cold. I was not familiar with croup, for none in my family had ever had it, but I was aware of its symptoms and potential danger as told to me by neighbors whose children suffered from it. Our heavenly Father was with us that winter, for the boys did not have croup or any severe colds at all. For the rest of their childhood, they did not ever again have the croup. My husband decided that the open air our house provided, albeit cold, was good for them!

My coming baby brought problems I had not experienced in my prior pregnancy. I was extremely depressed at times and physically tired more than I remembered from before. I had gained more weight and felt so unattractive. My husband did all he could to make me feel better about myself, but nothing worked. All in all, it was a difficult time for me, and I know it had to be for Brad, for he had to spend a lot of time reassuring me in my periods of depression. I tend to wonder what kind of mother I was for the children during this time; I honestly don't remember. I do know that I never resented having the sudden big family, and I even wonder now if having them around didn't help me through some of the difficulties I was experiencing.

My sweet little girl Kaylene, who was ten years old at that time, was such a wonderful help. She was good with the little ones and was always taking on a household chore so much bigger than her small frame should have handled. She was so eager to please me. After she was grown, I still felt guilty about the things I permitted her to do to help me, and I told her so.

She seemed astounded that I felt guilt, for she told me, "Mom, you have no reason to feel that way. You never made me do those things. I did them to please you, and you needed help!"

82

Six Plus Two

Baby Renee was born April 25, 1950. As my pregnancy with her had been, so was her birth—difficult. She came into the world, loudly protesting her entry, at a birth weight of eight pounds, fifteen ounces, a pound and a half larger than her sister Margene at birth. Renee suffered from a digestive disorder that caused her constant pain during the first three months or so of her life. She cried most all of the time, and all my doctor could say was that it would pass and to urge me to go on giving her a medication called paregoric. The medication had a calming effect on the child but, as I understand, can no longer be sold for children's use. I now know that the active ingredient is tincture of opium, a narcotic. It worked for Renee, but only for short periods of time. At some time during the treatment of my baby, the doctor withdrew his prescription (or recommendation, whichever it was; I don't recall whether it was a prescription or over-the-counter medication).

Time changes a lot of rules to be followed in rearing a baby, it seems. Just recently, in a box of pictures, I found an article about child rearing that was apparently clipped from a magazine in the 1950s. Actually, it was only part of an article, for the clipping's intended side for use was a coupon for cloth baby diapers, expiration date May 31, 1950. The partial article on the reverse side advised a new father that in the event he might have to babysit, he might want to take up a hobby to pass the time, for he should only "pick up the baby when the baby needed to be fed or its diaper changed or was being hurt, perhaps by a sticking pin or too-tight clothing." Apparently, the author felt that to pick it up otherwise was not healthy for the baby; therefore, supposedly, a father taking care of a baby would find he had a lot of time on his hands.

My point for the foregoing is that some of the methods for child rearing today are far distant from the ones I thought to be the proper ones when my children were babies! Things and methods change and sometimes do complete reversals over time.

When my little one finally outgrew her months of colic, she began to develop a distinct personality—fun loving and mischievous! Even though we expected that the indigestion from the colic and her inability to eat as a baby might serve to set her back in growth and development, it didn't happen. She had rapidly regained the lost time and caught up to normal size and development expected in a child of her age. In her eleventh month, she began to walk, and shortly after she became thirteen months old, she was roller-skating! Granted, her style was a little different from the older children; instead of skating forward in a straight path, she skated in a circle using only one foot to propel herself. When she finally realized that to go forward she would have to use the other foot, as well, then she mastered it. She easily caught on to games requiring physical activities as a child.

She seemed to excel in many areas from toddler to preteen. She could sing in such a clear, beautiful voice even as a young child and could play a piano without knowledge of music or benefit of lessons. She excelled at storytelling and kept children, other family members, and relatives entertained for hours with her stories and dialects.

In later years, our family performed professionally as the Brad Carrington Water Ski Troupe, and Renee was, unquestionably, the star of our show. Later, our little Leeza, the second from last of our children, grew into the starring role of the ski troupe (by that time, Mr. Stork was competing with us, and Renee had given up the starring role to take on another role, that of wife and mother!). Our daughter Margene had briefly dropped out for the same reason the season before.

Thirteen months after Renee was born on April 25, 1951, the Carrington family again saw an increase in the size of the family. Our little redhead Leeza was born, weighing in at six pounds, nine ounces.

Only thirteen months between the babies had caused an increase of two children to our family in little more than a year, so to offset the expense of another child, an increase of income for Brad in his job situation was needed badly. Fortunately, the mines were producing more and more coal as new sites opened up. One of their sites due west up on the mountain from us, with its entryway directly across the highway from the driveway of our home, was the site where Brad worked. His job was still dozer operator with a second job as hauler for them, but in any spare time he could squeeze in, he still kept buying and selling coal from that site. Its close location saved travel downtime, as he practically lived on the site. He could make as much and more money with less time away from home, and not only did we catch up financially but we were able to save a little for the future, despite our rapidly increasing family.

83

A Dreaded Fear Springs to Life

Overloaded trucks continually came off the hill, and I always worried about a runaway coming across the highway and into our yard, even though our house sat back from the road a couple of hundred feet, which Brad felt was enough of a buffer zone to be safe from that danger. However, I didn't want the children to play in the front because of that. As the summer became quite warm, the cool shade of an ancient Kentucky coffee bean tree was enticing for the boys, and they played in the dirt under that tree with their toy trucks and dozers. The tree had such dense foliage that no grass would grow under it, and the bare, loose soil there made the ideal place for the boys to play in the dirt—not my choice as an ideal play area for them, however, but I conceded.

The coffee tree stood about twenty-five feet from the house, and I could watch them as they played. One day, shortly after I had called the children in for lunch, we suddenly heard the blasts from an air horn coming rapidly closer and then a crash. It had happened. A truck had run away, and the old coffee tree had stopped it. I learned later that coming through the lawn had slowed down the truck and that the collision with the tree did little damage. The scary thing, though, was that minutes before, our little boys had been playing just a few feet from where the truck stopped with the old tree between the loaded coal truck and their toys! God was truly with us that day!

That runaway was the only one coming into our yard while we lived there. The steep part of the mountain is where runaways normally happened, and the drivers were able to slow down as the hill leveled out, which it did considerably a long way before reaching the highway.

We could tell when something happened at the mine or on the road leading into or out of it by the traffic flow. Also, by watching the order of the trucks going in before or behind Brad when he was hauling, we knew when to expect him out, and I would plan dinner accordingly.

The scary thing about watching the trucks flow on these busy hauling evenings, though, was when we saw that trucks that had followed Brad's truck in were coming out before him! One or two trucks may be out of line but never a string of them without there being something wrong. Trucks did break down, and occasionally, a longer-than-normal delay would result when a truck turned over. And since this continued after the mountain was pitch black at night, the only light being the machinery and truck lights, it was not unusual for a heavily loaded truck to back into a deeper-than-normal rut, and the heavy load would cause the truck to break a drive shaft or axle and sometimes even overturn. If Brad did have a breakdown that could hold him longer than normal (he rolled his truck once), some of the other drivers would come into our driveway to let me know that he was okay but temporarily delayed. The drivers were all local men; they knew each other and looked out for one another.

84

Rare Summer Leisure

In the spring of 1951, we were better off financially than we had ever been. Brad had been working so hard for the past four years, and finally, we were even able to add to our small savings. Brad began to take off on Sundays, and we would all would go to church and then do something enjoyable as a family for the rest of the day. Leisure time was a new concept for us. Brad's brother Daniel and he had bought an old fishing boat, cut it down, and remade it into a boat that, as he and Daniel hoped, would be a great boat for water-skiing. Now, the two of them wouldn't know a water ski if they saw one except for what they had seen in the comic section of the newspaper. No one in our area seemed to know what they were. This was in the early season of the appearance of TVA (Tennessee Valley Authority) lakes that were being built on rivers in southern Kentucky and in Tennessee. When those lakes started to appear, so did the popularity of water sports, making all types of water sports equipment a more common sight. However, at the time the brothers were dreaming and experimenting was just prior to the time that water-skiing equipment was commonplace in our area of Kentucky.

Brad and Daniel set out to make a set of water skis. Their plan was to experiment until they were able to make a pair that a man could ride, and then they could work on child-sized ones for the kids. The first set was about eight feet long and ten inches wide by three-quarters of an inch thick. They knew the front of the ski should turn up, but not being able to figure out how to make wood bend, they cut the wood and made the turn-up angle from two pieces of wood bracketed into an angle that looked about right. They had no idea where the foot piece should go, so they held off on that until they could get to a lake to experiment.

Since I was not with them when they launched their inventions, I cannot ever imagine, even after hearing their versions of the day, how things transpired. Apparently, though, after figuring out where to put the shoes (yes, they used an old pair of cast-off men's shoes for the binders) on the barn-door-like boards meant for water skis, they decided it was time for the first trial. They tried to ride these strange-looking slabs behind the fishing/ski boat and met failure after failure. I can imagine the whooping and hollering when one of them finally got up and rode around just a little before the skis with the added weight of one of the men almost capsized the boat.

That's when a fisherman came over to them, and after he realized the contraptions they were hauling through the water were meant to be water skis, he told them he had seen some in Florida. "And they sure didn't look like those. They were no longer than four or five feet," he said.

He also told them he had seen a boatbuilder put a curve in wood by applying steam to the wood and putting it in a brace to curve it.

Armed with this new information, the guys began to put their heads together to come up with a method where, with their limited equipment, they could channel steam to be concentrated enough to put the bend in their skis— and then there was the problem of just how long theirs should be. I honestly don't know how they finally did come up with the set that worked, but they did! I know the second set, at four feet in length, was too short and the set that worked was longer and the tips were curved—not exactly in matching curves, but they worked. This was several weeks' worth of trial and failure before success, but they soon decided against an assembly line for their product. A short time later, they found that a well-known mail-order supplier had water skis in their catalog, and voilà! The Brad Carrington Water Ski Troupe was born! (It was years later before the troupe actually materialized, however.)

Daniel had grown tired of boating for water sports and had chosen to do serious fishing. Brad's interest in the sports was mainly that he was working toward finding something for the family as a whole to enjoy together. The children had already shown an avid interest in boating, swimming, and camping, though—as our family was still growing—we didn't get to spend much time off the farm to camp. We did boat a lot that spring, however, and our kids all learned to swim.

We had finally gotten our successfully converted fishing/water-ski boat performing just like we wanted, and I loved to ride in it. However, I was getting so cumbersome with my late-term pregnancy that I found it hard to get in and out of the boat. Brad finally solved the problem by putting me in the boat and telling me to stay there. After he had learned to ski and ride another homemade item that we termed a "surfboard" and later found out its proper name was "aquaplane," he taught other friends at the lake on both pieces of equipment. It was extremely enjoyable for me to ride and, from the boat, watch all the activities.

I had so enjoyed the day! In the first place, Brad's newly married sister Treena had offered to give me some time off by watching my kids for the day, a definite treat for me. At the end of the day, I was relaxed, happy, and very sleepy. By the time we had loaded the boat and returned to Treena's house, it was after nine o'clock. She told us she had fed and bathed the kids and put them to bed, suggesting we leave them there for the night. Brad thought it best that we do, and I didn't argue, even though it was such a rarity for Brad to agree to allow the kids to stay away from home overnight anywhere. I was glad, for I was very tired. We went home and went directly to bed. I don't even remember undressing.

85

A Surprise Arrival

At about midnight, I awakened from a deep sleep thinking that a hot liquid was being poured over my midsection. However, the sensation was gone by the time I was fully awake. Thinking it a dream, I turned over to go back to sleep when it came again. It was then I realized I was in labor, and the pains were one right after the other! We got my ready-packed suitcase, jumped into the car, and headed for the hospital. On the way to the hospital, I can only recall having a solid wave of pain with no letup. Upon arrival, I told the nurse I thought the baby was coming, for by then, I felt extreme pressure and the need to push, and I told her so. I begged her to please call my doctor. She only laughed at me and said, "You've got lots of time. We haven't even prepped you yet. Besides, he's in the hospital; we can call him when we need him."

She urged me to lie back and relax, saying, "When the time comes, we will call the doctor, but that's a while yet. In the meantime, I will get a nurses' helper in here to prep you."

I again begged her to call the doctor, because I thought the baby was coming. As she left the room, she told me that she would when it was closer to time. I only vaguely remember the nurse assistant coming into the room. I was in a solid wall of pain. I remember her pulling up my gown and, with a loud gasp, yelling for the nurse. I remember nothing else, and thirty minutes later (they told me the time the next day), I awakened to Brad smoothing my hair from my face and kissing my forehead as he told me we had a little redhead who was in a hurry to come.

All I could think to say was, "They haven't even prepped me yet!"

Little redheaded Leeza gave me the easiest pregnancy and the shortest labor I have ever had. I had no stitches, no aftereffects, no itching from prepping, nothing to make recovery long, painful, or uncomfortable. She caused no interruption to my life, it seemed. To further make the point, I was back on the lake and back in the boat (I could climb in and out with ease), and I did get out to go back to my family and to feed my new baby, who was being cuddled by Ma, as she had accompanied us to the lake to help take care of the kids. She worried about them around water, she would tell us. Little did any of us know that our kids would spend a lot of their growing-up years around water!

86

Baby Leeza

I had tried breast-feeding with my first baby, Margene, and had not been successful. The baby did not suffer from my attempt, but I think my youth and impatience were the reasons my milk would just not come down. The hungry cry of my baby was something that served to increase my impatience, so I could not relax enough for it to be successful. I hadn't even tried it with my second baby, Renee. However, I carried a guilt complex about it, and because I felt so well after my easy experience of birthing Leeza, I felt a need to breast-feed her. After a month, I realized she wasn't growing, but I was sure she was getting enough milk, for, as per the doctor's instructions, I had pumped and measured. She began to spit up, and it was obvious her stomach was hurting. Her cry started to sound less like a baby and more like the cry of a kitten. The bones in her face and chest had become so prominent, and her arms and legs were so thin. Her stomach seemed to be getting larger.

In the first week of August, when she was six weeks old, I knew something was very wrong, and I took my baby to the doctor. He took one look and said, "Your baby is badly malnourished," and after thoroughly examining her, he told me to take her away from all milk for three days. I was instructed to put her on a mixture of a clear carbonated beverage and water for the three days and to bring her back on the fourth day. During days she was not nursing, I was to pump and measure the breast milk as regularly as I had fed the baby before and keep an accurate measurement of the amount of milk I pumped.

"And," he stressed, "no way are you to feed the baby any of the milk; feed her only the soda and water!" He gave instructions to the nurse to set up an early-morning appointment for us to return.

The next three days were so hard. I didn't know how the little one could live on soda and water, without milk, for she was so thin and so sick. However, she soon began to feel better. Her constant crying had stopped, the diarrhea had gone away, and she didn't look so pale.

The doctor looked pleased as he started to examine her. He said, "The amount of milk you have pumped and measured is adequate, but I suspect your milk has no strength. I am going to place her on a formula, and after she becomes accustomed to it, I believe she will thrive." He started her on a diluted formula, which she took like a hungry kitten. In a few days, as instructed, I mixed the formula normally and she had no problems.

She immediately began to make progress. She needed more milk, and I gradually increased the amount I fed her. By the middle of September, she was just a little under the place on the expected growth scale she should have been at three months old. I was so thankful to our heavenly Father for bringing our beautiful baby girl back from the downhill slide she was in just a month before.

Other than my baby's slow growth and malnutrition, which was discovered in time for a correction before it was critical, the summer of 1951 was a good summer. We were financially sound, and since Brad didn't have to work so much, he had given up his two jobs with the stripping company and taken over the free enterprise of a welding and repair shop with a contract to take care of the heavy equipment of the same stripping company for whom he had worked as an employee. They were glad to have a repair shop close by to take in parts for welding and repair, especially one where they could take in large mobile equipment. Brad soon began to get all the work he could handle and even hired an apprentice to help with the repair.

87

All is Well

Where Brad had worked two and three jobs before, this one job often filled the time of three! However, we still found time to do things as a family, for he tried to leave Sundays free. We were both so proud of our family. The kids were happy and watched over each other so well that we were able to take them places, and it was so good to be together. After our little Leeza started to grow again, our worries were so much less than they had ever been before. Little did we realize the change that was coming!

88

Danger on the Mountain

As autumn of 1951 approached, there began to be more and more demand on Brad's time, and many times, he was up on the mountain alone after operations closed down for the night. When I knew the mines had closed and he had not come home, I stood at the window watching for truck lights that I would know to be his coming down off the mountain, and on many of those nights, I would go to bed long before he finished the job.

One night while welding under a dozer, Brad realized the fuel gauge on his gasoline-powered welder was on empty and that he would soon have to stop. He had a little more to weld before he finished the job, and rather than stopping his work to go back to his garage for more gasoline, he filled his five-gallon can by siphoning some from the tank of the gasoline-powered dozer.

It was necessary for him to climb up on the dozer to get to the tank opening. When he got the siphon going, he realized the gasoline would be running very slowly, and he decided to go down to weld a little more while the can was filling. Apparently, more time had passed than he realized when he saw that a stream of gasoline had run into the area close to where he was welding. He immediately knew that the can had run over!

Just as Brad discovered the overflow, it made contact with a live spark from his welding and caught fire. He ran to stamp out the fire and managed to extinguish the flame but in the process caught the legs of his pants on fire. He quickly got away from the gasoline for fear it would reignite or that the fumes would blow. The process of running fanned the flames on his clothing, and by then, they had really flared up. When he felt that he was far enough away, he did lie down and roll until the fire was out. A lot of his pants legs were burned, and in the process, he had some burns on his legs. He was aware the fumes could still ignite at any moment and could reach him.

It was then that he uttered a prayer—"Please, God, help me!" His prayer was answered, and he saw no more flames.

89

Nighttime Vulnerability

The close call with fire that could have been fatal had made Brad rethink working alone on the mountain and putting himself in such a position of danger. Fire was only one of the dangers he faced when working on or around heavy equipment, for sometimes he had to depend on jacks he doubted were sturdy enough to handle the load and then had to crawl under this equipment thus supported. He began to question whether or not he wanted to place himself and his family in the precarious position he did when he went out on these jobs. During the time he was examining himself, he wanted to talk to me about it but didn't want me to worry while he was still doing that kind of job. I could be quite a worrywart about a lot less. I would worry even more if I had known that kind of thing was happening. The fire I knew about; how could he hide burned-off pants legs and burned legs?

Another night in November, Brad had gone up on the mountain to weld and repair a large dozer, and because he was about to refuse the job, the company had agreed to have two men stay and help with the grunt work. He had agreed to go and had been gone since early evening. It was well after midnight, and I kept going to the window to watch for him. I did so want him safe at home! My stirring around had awakened the baby, and I picked her up and took her to the window. I needed to hold my baby for the comfort her warm little body would give me. I knew I wouldn't be able to sleep; I was missing him so much! The moon was full and was what we called a harvest moon. Back in the day when Brad was working one shift and coming home, we had time to go for walks, and one of our favorite times was to walk under a full moon, particularly the harvest moon. I yearned for a chance to hold hands and walk with him that night, but we had so little time for *us* in those days. With poignant memories in my mind, I started to cry, and it was then that I realized how sensitive babies are to our feelings; her little face was puckered to cry because I was crying. I hugged her to me and worked to get myself under control while murmuring soothing sounds to my child to put her at ease.

It was nearly five in the morning when Brad finally came home and got into bed. He asked me to wake him at seven, for he had to be back at the garage at seven thirty. It was this way for the next few months, and Brad was looking very tired much of the time.

90

Indications of Trouble

On two occasions that winter, when I took lunch to Brad while he was working in the garage, I found him sitting behind the little potbellied stove, his source of heat for the garage. The first time that I had walked in on him, he had a small pad of paper and a very short pencil.

Once before when I had noticed his two-inch pencil, I had offered to get him a longer one, and he refused, saying, "I can easily carry this one around in my pocket."

This time, when I asked him what he was doing, he looked up, startled (he hadn't heard me come in), and then I noticed how worried he looked. He answered, "Oh, just trying to figure out how to make a dollar."

I was to hear these words a number of times throughout our life together, and he was always able to find the answer. I noticed, upon looking around, that he had several unfinished jobs sitting there. I asked if he was waiting for parts. He answered, "No, I'm getting to them." That, somehow, did not ring true.

During the winter, available jobs seemed to be more slowly coming in. I thought the reason was that the roads to the strip mines were impassable many days because of the weather. I later found that it was more than the weather.

Brad had gotten all the repair work caught up on the equipment that was in his garage and was having days with very little to do. Fortunately, in his thrifty way, he had put aside money to tide us over for times like that. I'm sure he worried, though he never told me so. If I asked, his answer would be, "We'll be all right. Don't you worry!"

In February 1952, I found that I was again pregnant, and with the current state of our slow economy, I wondered if Brad might become even more worried with this news of a coming child to further increase our large family. He never made me feel like he didn't want another child or that being pregnant was in any way something I could have avoided. I know that his brother Daniel often razzed him about "overdoing this family thing" and, in very crude language, what should be done about it.

91

Lessons Learned

Brad continued to go out for the on-site repair jobs but limited them to daytime and to only those jobs that could not be moved to his garage. At night, he worked on equipment that was brought to him. It was on some of the long evenings when he was working at the garage that I sat at the kitchen window and watched from the house for his welding flare. Somehow, just seeing that flare made me feel closer to him. I got to see him so little, and I missed him so much.

Our baby Leeza had finally begun to fill out and grow. Her easy entry into this world had turned into a not-so-easy first few months for the little one.

In late winter of 1952, I had gotten so busy with painting the house, as Brad had finally finished the inside walls, that I had gotten into the habit of putting the baby down with a bottle. She was in her crib in the living room just around the corner from where I was working in the kitchen and other rooms that were nearby. I would look in, occasionally, to check her progress on the bottle I had given her. I had put Renee down for her nap at the same time as the baby. The other little one, Margene, who was too young to go to school, played alone in the corner. It would then be quiet enough for Leeza and Renee to get a long nap. Many times when I checked, Leeza had emptied her bottle but was still sucking it and almost asleep. I took the empty away and made a mental note to increase the milk, because it was gone too soon, which should mean she needed more. Even after having increased the milk, she still seemed to be emptying her bottle too quickly; I even looked for leakage! Not at the beginning but later on, she started acting hungry just after having a bottle, her weight gain had stopped, and she was crying more. She was even beginning to look thin again.

One day, I had put both Renee and Leeza down for a nap, as usual, and the baby with a bottle (Renee had been weaned earlier). I was in the kitchen making preparation for dinner, and I heard the baby's bottle fall to the floor. I popped around the corner to pick it up and saw Renee scurrying from under the baby bed with the bottle, saying, "I put it back!" I took the bottle from her, and realizing it was empty, I looked at Renee, who had a ring of milk around her mouth with fresh bubbles in the milk.

I accusingly asked, "Did you drink the baby's milk?"

She looked as if she were going to cry, saying, "I help, I help!"

Then I realized just what had been going on and could not believe I hadn't caught her before then. She was drinking the baby's milk! I realized, also, if I was going to give my youngest child a chance to grow and be healthy, I had to take better care of her.

I started holding the baby to feed her and could almost see her grow. I had been depriving myself, as well as the baby, by *not* holding her when she was being fed, for there's a lot of pleasure to be had in holding your baby. I didn't stop to think then and I realize now as I write this, Renee was just a baby too. She had been weaned at thirteen months, just before Leeza was born, but she was still in diapers until shortly before the bottle-stealing period. She really didn't get to be the baby long enough and was hurting because of it. You know how they say hindsight is twenty-twenty. Needless to say, I did start giving Renee more milk. Where were the sippy cups then? Dee, who lived just up the road from me, made up somewhat for my lack of time for Renee. She cuddled her a lot, as Renee seemed to cry excessively and was going through some very rough periods. Her early babyhood digestive problem seemed to have returned. She was a happy little girl for the most part though.

92

Three Nannies and a Cantankerous Billy

Summer was a busy time for me with the children home from school and the garden to take care of along with the preserving of its bounty. Brad gave me all the assistance he could but was pretty busy himself, "trying to make a dollar." We had a cow that I milked twice daily, which kept a plentiful supply of cow's milk available for the family. However, because of the problems Renee and Leeza had with their stomachs, we had gotten a goat to try goat's milk to replace the cow's milk in their diets. It seemed to help. Brad preferred to drink goat's milk also, and we decided to keep a few goats for milking.

Of course, if you have nannies (female goats), that meant in order to keep fresh milk, we would eventually need a billy (male goat) for our females. Brad bought one and brought the billy home. That was the beginning of a whole new problem for me. We could not keep the billy penned. He would climb over any fence, no matter how high we made it. If we kept him in the barn, he would stand and butt the door until his horn sockets would be bloody. If we put a collar on him, he would pull on it until he broke it. We finally tried putting the rope around his horns, and when he found out pulling on it gave him too much discomfort, he would chew on the rope until he would again be loose. The children were very afraid of the billy, for he would butt anything that moved.

Any time the billy broke loose, he had to be caught and again restrained. I, being the only adult home and eight months pregnant, had to be the one to catch him and hold him until one of the boys could get the rope (or whatever we were currently using to restrain him) around his neck or his horns. To catch him, I only had to go toward him, and he would *run* toward me, head lowered. I then had to catch him by the horns just before he plowed into me and hold on. Simple, huh? As I grabbed him, I had to sidestep, dig in my heels, and hold on to stop his momentum; otherwise, my baby bump would take the blow. Luckily, he was not very big, but he was very strong for his size. The next hurdle, then, was to coax my eight-year-old Brad Jr. to come to me with the restraint and put it around his neck until I could pen him or whatever I could do with him to keep him from running loose and butting everyone or everything that moved.

All the while, I was trying to coax my son to bring the restraint, but it took a bit of time, for Brad Jr. was very scared, and during that time, the goat was trying to butt me in the stomach. By the time my son was convinced I would not let go, I was so tired I was not really sure that I *could* hold on! He finally did get the courage to bring the goat's restraint, and I could then pen the goat. During the day, this happened repeatedly. Then one day, after catching and penning the goat four times, I was done with him. I finally put him in the barn to let him butt and bloody his horns until they were torn off for all I cared! When Brad came home, he told me he would get rid of him the next day.

The very next day, a man from over the mountain came to look at the billy and said he wanted to buy him but would have to come back the next day with the money. Brad didn't want the goat to stay around until the next day and told him to take the goat with him that night and bring the money the next day.

The man came back the next day as promised and reported, "The goat I was going to buy is dead. I was just leading him, and he was always pulling back and stopping, so when he dropped dead, I just thought he was up to his tricks. This time, he didn't get up when I yanked the rope! He was deader'n a doornail."

At this point, he pulled out the money he would have owed for the goat and said, "Here's the money. Now you owe me a goat."

Brad, refusing the money, said, "I only had the one billy, so you will have to buy one somewhere else." We were so happy to have the goat gone that we really didn't care if it happened the way the man said or not. Brad believed the man might have become so angry with the cantankerous goat that he may have beaten it to death!

93

A Kick into Oblivion

One of the chores I completed twice daily was milking our cow for the family milk. Brad Jr. was my little helper in all the chores and would go with me and put out the grain and hay for the cow while I milked, and he would stay with me until I finished. One day, when the cow came into the area where I milked her, he noticed that she had a large swollen place on her bag just above one of her teats. I sent Brad Jr. across the road to ask if the neighboring farmer would walk over to look at our cow. He was not a veterinarian but was good with animal ailments. He came and looked at the wound and announced that he believed it to be a snakebite, which often happened, he told us. He suggested an ointment to use to treat it. He assured us that there would be no reason we could not use the milk, just not from that teat. But he cautioned us that, even though we were not to use it, we should make sure that the teat was cleanly stripped. (The process of going back over after milking and getting all the milk possible out of each teat was called "stripping." If this is not done with each milking, a form of mastitis develops, which results in a decrease in milk production and can possibly result in a permanent situation with the animal.) The main ingredient in the salve we used on the cow's injury/infection was carbolic acid, a product the kids continued to call "cow salve" throughout their growing-up years. It was an ointment sold by a door-to-door salesman of a company that specialized in pharmaceuticals intended for human use. We were to find that it worked equally well for minor infections on both humans and animals.

After our farmer neighbor left, I did my usual milking, leaving her sore teat for last. As I began to milk it, she reacted immediately to the pain. I carefully milked it and was making progress, but I must have gotten a little rough with her for, suddenly, she kicked, hitting me hard on the side of my head. Her blow knocked me off the milk stool and over the edge of the ridge I sat on, and I ended up about ten feet downhill from the stool. I must have lost consciousness momentarily, for the next thing I remember is Brad Jr. leaning over me, crying and trying to lift me into a sitting position. I had a raised knot on my head, but I was all right otherwise. I reassured my little boy, and he helped me put a hobble (a gadget designed to make a cow unable to kick) on the cow, and I finished stripping her. For the next few days, Brad made sure he didn't schedule anything at milking time and did the milking himself. It turned out to be more than a few days, for I ended up being off longer than expected.

94

Behind Closed Doors

The month of September had slipped up on me, but it was more than welcome. I was so glad to have cooler weather, for summer pregnancies were killers! Along with the uncomfortable heat, I was beginning to have some problems with severe vertigo that seemed to be getting increasingly worse and was causing extreme nausea. On September 3 after my checkup appointment, the doctor wanted to put me in the hospital, as he was concerned about my vertigo and nausea. I was beginning to have lots of pain in my stomach and horrible constipation as well. After a day of testing, the doctor determined that my problems were coming from the iron and possibly other minerals in the concentrated vitamin mix I had been taking; consequently, he took me off them. I was so run down that he wanted me to stay in the hospital a few days longer so that they could concentrate on getting me ready and able to have my baby.

I was released on September 10 to go home and was cautioned to get a lot of rest. I was home on the eleventh, and very early on September 12, I went into labor and was back in the hospital. I was in labor eleven hours, and no progress was made at all. The maternity ward staff told me they would give me a little more time, and if nothing happened, they would induce labor. I was in such severe pain, which felt as if a door inside of me was closed and lots of pressure seemed to be against that closed door. I don't know what caused that feeling, for they never explained it to me, and I had not had it with any of the other births. Then the labor pain became more intense, and still that door would not open. Once, after an examination by the nurse, they conferred, and someone went after the doctor. After his examination, he came to talk to me. He told me I was about to have the baby but that the baby was not in the correct position to go into the birth canal and that he would have to turn it before I could birth it. (I say "it," for in those days, doctors could not tell the sex of the baby prior to birth as they do today.)

I was in and out of consciousness as the nurse had injected something she said was to control the pain. I seemed to come wide awake as the nurse was gently squeezing my shoulder and asking me if my husband was in the hospital. I said that he was, and she left. She came back shortly with Brad and told me the doctor wanted to talk to both of us. I was puzzled, thinking, *Why am I not having the baby?* The doctor came in and said that we needed to talk about something that needed a decision from us and it needed to be made immediately. You can imagine all the things that ran through my mind and consequently how scared I was.

95

Our Warning; My Surprise

Dr. Smittie was an older and very trusted doctor at Denton's only hospital, and he had been the doctor to deliver all my children. He knew us well, and we respected and trusted him. He started pointing out different problems I had had with this pregnancy, the hospitalization for the fatigue, and the difficult times I had during labor (at that point, I remember thinking that whatever the nurse had given me for pain had helped, for I felt no pain). He went on to say that there had been a problem that I didn't even know about and that was that my placenta had grown to my womb. He further told us that, when that happened, the next pregnancy could even be worse, for he had seen cases where the fetus itself had grown to the womb, and that was often life threatening for either or both the mother and baby. Once these problems happened, they were more than likely to continue with each subsequent pregnancy.

Dr. Smittie continued, "You have a large family already by today's standards. Don't you feel that you have enough? And given the situations I've just pointed out, I would like to make a recommendation. Now, while Rachel is in the hospital, would be an excellent time for us to perform a surgical procedure on her to prevent future pregnancies."

Brad spoke for the first time then. He said, "I don't want her to have that surgery, for I have heard that it's hard on a woman's body later. I have also heard there's something that you can do to a man that will make it not possible for him to get his wife pregnant and that it's easier on a man than the surgery for a woman. Can you tell us anything about that?"

Dr. Smittie answered, "Yes. I've performed that procedure. It's very simple, recovery time is short, and the man suffers no long-term effect from the surgery. The only condition I must warn about would be the psychological effect it could have if the man should dwell on the fact he can no longer father children. Other cases would be where a man remarries, in smaller families where he should lose a child, or in other cases where the man is not psychologically strong. I don't think any of these reasons apply to you.

Yes, that would be my suggested route. I'll have to say, however, it's not often that the male volunteers! That's what you're doing, isn't it?"

"Yes. Tell me what's going to happen and when you'll do it."

The doctor winked at me and said, "Good man you got here!" And to Brad, he said, "It doesn't have to be tonight. We just have to make sure it's done before she gets pregnant again, and with you two, that isn't long. I'm going to keep her in the hospital a few days, and it can't happen here." He chuckled. "I would suggest that we talk within the next two weeks and set a date. In the meantime, I'll give you a pamphlet; look it over, and if you have any questions, we'll discuss them when we get together again."

All the time they were talking, I was getting quite anxious. *What about my baby?! Have I had it?* The nurses seemed to be busily cleaning the maternity room, and there was no baby in sight. Brad saw me looking around and knew I was anxious about something.

He squeezed my hand and said, "We've got ourselves a perfect little blonde baby girl! She's beautiful."

A nurse, hearing our conversation, asked, "Would you like to hold her?" Breathing a sigh of relief, I exclaimed, "Yes!"

The nurse disappeared behind a curtain, and I briefly heard sounds of babies crying. She was back in just a moment with my beautiful little girl Eileen, with a card pinned to her blanket stating, "Carrington Girl, BD: 9/12/52, 7 lb. 2 oz." She was perfect!

All my other babies were born with red marks on their foreheads, just above the nose; Eileen didn't have this. I later asked the doctor the reason they all had it and she did not. He suggested I look on the back of her head. They were there! He went on to say that Eileen's placement during birth was not the natural one of the baby facing the front, but her position was that she faced my spinal column. This position caused a more difficult birth, as I had experienced. The other ones got pressure from a part of my body, causing the spots to appear on their faces and on the back of Eileen's head. (I have found that the red marks do disappear with time; well, almost, anyway!)

96

The Magic Number Is Seven

Going home from the hospital was rather scary, for I felt so tired. I needn't have worried, however, for Brad had gotten me help. I was covered! My sister Josie met me at the car with my baby Leeza in her arms. They were "besties," Josie and "Meesh" (Josie's pet name for my little girl). My sixteen-year-old sister Shar peeked out the door with a potato and paring knife in her hand. Someone was cooking; I wondered who. As I entered my kitchen, dear Mama took a smoking-hot skillet out of the oven and poured in the makings for corn bread. I smelled cabbage (one of the vegetables still available from the garden). If that was all she had prepared, that would have been just fine, for I loved cooked cabbage and corn bread—and so did Brad. Actually, they had a late-garden feast prepared for my homecoming. And as I have said before, I love to eat!

Josie had her boyfriend's car and had brought Mama and Shar out to our farm and was to take Mama home. Mama said, "If you need her, I will leave Shar here to help you for a week or so." I was so glad to have this little sister stay—not only to help but because I enjoyed being with her. She was so helpful and always so pleasant.

Vividly, I recall an incident on the occasion of this stay in September 1952. We still had corn in the garden, and Shar loved corn. If there was anything we had in the fall tasting better than corn to Shar, it was Concord grapes! When corn was in season, I served it for almost every dinner. Until cold weather came, the grapes were always there for the picking. And Shar picked! Not being accustomed to eating many grapes and not having lots of corn for meals, as living on a farm provides, Shar just ate too much of both. She developed an upset stomach accompanied by diarrhea, causing her to be miserable.

She didn't want anyone to know, especially me, so she tried to help as much as she had been doing in the past. Potato peeling was always something she did for me, and she was getting it done. I was mixing the bread and just happened to look over at Shar. She had her head down on the table and was deathly white, but she was still peeling potatoes. I loved her so much at that moment; I wanted nothing more than to hug that little girl! Being that in those days my family was not very demonstrative and as it tended to create great embarrassment for both the giver and receiver, I refrained and just told her to go lie down until supper was ready and that she didn't have to help until she was over the stomach upset. She was sick another day, but that didn't stop her from helping.

When Eileen was a week old, Brad injured his back while lifting an acetylene tank in his welding shop. At that time, he hadn't made his arrangements for the surgical procedure the doctor had recommended, and having to take off work because of his back, he called and set up to see the doctor for his back and for the procedure the doctor had recommended—a vasectomy—on the same day in order to have less time off work. As continued throughout his working career, Brad would not miss work, unless he just couldn't possibly get there. The doctor jokingly called him a glutton for punishment, but in reality, that was just how my practical husband always handled things. He was off two days after his minor surgery, and another pregnancy was no longer a worry. Our family was to stop at seven children.

97

Stockpiling

Later, toward spring, I noticed that Brad was clearing off the land lying directly behind his welding shop, and I asked him if he planned to plant it. He said he was thinking about buying some coal and piling it there to sell to those who needed coal for the winter; there were still housewives who cooked with coal for fuel.

He continued, "I can buy coal at a low price right now and should be able to make money later with it." He had bought and sold coal earlier, before he started hauling exclusively for the company, but he hadn't done it for a while.

I asked, "When do you think you will have any time to do that?"

He said, "I'm thinking about cutting back the welding work and getting into something else."

I was glad to hear that but a little worried about the reasons. Without his telling me anything that should worry me, for some unexplained reason, I *was* worried. It was what he wasn't telling me that had me concerned.

As he had said he would, Brad started stockpiling coal, even selling loads from time to time right out of his truck before bringing it to the lot. When he had his lot full, he began to build a piece of equipment that, when finished, he could use to load his truck without the backbreaking job of shoveling it on. It was a type of electric-powered elevator.

As Brad emptied a spot in his coal yard, he would buy more and fill the empty spot. Later, I noticed he had a big spot empty that grew bigger as he sold, with none being hauled in to replace it.

I asked, "Why aren't you buying more to fill the empty spot?"

"I don't want to get too far ahead until I know I'm going to need more," Brad answered.

It made sense, so his answer satisfied me; however, I feared he might be getting low on funds that would be needed to buy more.

98

A Near Tragedy

Our new little one, Eileen, didn't seem to have the colic and various baby disorders the other little ones had in their early months. Actually, she just seemed to delay these maladies until she was in her teens. It was then that she seemed to be more susceptible to stomach upset than she was as a baby.

Eileen grew rapidly, and since there was a little more than fourteen months in age between Eileen and Leeza, when Eileen started to walk, she was almost as big as her sister Leeza. The two were inseparable as children, and even now, though they are both in their sixties, they—as well as their husbands—are still very close. They were the same size most of their lives. Even though they did not look alike, people would often ask me if they were twins.

Leeza sucked her thumb. I would notice that it wasn't a constant thing, but when she had the urge to suck it, she would anxiously look around until she found her favorite dolly, a soft, bedraggled rag doll in a blue flour-sack dress (Ma had made it for her). She'd hug that doll up close, put her thumb in her mouth, curl her index finger around her nose, and begin to suck and walk— more of an amble than a walk. I don't know if she even watched where she was going; I would guess she was daydreaming or maybe drowsy from the comforting effect of sucking and the comfort of her doll. We had to watch her closely when she started to amble, because she would go where she didn't usually venture when she had her dolly and her thumb. As I mentioned before, we lived on a major highway with lots of truck traffic.

Our children had a healthy fear of the highway, and never did we have to worry about them venturing onto the road. We never thought that it could become a worry to us.

One day, when Leeza was a little less than two years old, Brad came home from his garage and told me he was going into town to get some welding supplies and wanted to know if I needed anything. Realizing this would be a good opportunity to get in some groceries, I decided to go with him. I could shop while he went to pick up his welding supplies. We left the little ones, Margene, Renee, Leeza, and four-month-old Eileen for Kaylene to watch. Kaylene was a very trustworthy little twelve-year-old girl, and when she was given a duty to perform, especially if it involved the little ones, we never worried when she was in charge. The baby had just been fed and put down for what was usually a long nap, and Kaylene's monitoring would primarily consist of the other three little girls. The boys needed shoes and were going with us.

Apparently, that day when we left the house, Leeza left it too, close behind us, and Kaylene had not immediately discovered it. Suddenly, while still inside the living room of our house, Kaylene heard the blasts of air horns and the squealing of brakes coming from down the road a short distance. She looked out the door and saw Leeza ambling, her thumb in her mouth and her doll in her arms, right down the very middle of the highway!

The truck Kaylene had heard was stopped, and she could see on the other side of the road the owner of the grocery store, Jack Barnes, hurrying out toward the road and our little girl. Kaylene took off across a small hay field at a sprint toward her as well.

Later, while piecing together what happened, we learned from the driver of the truck that he was only a short distance back from where he had gotten his rig stopped when he had seen the baby in the road. He said, "Thank the Good Lord that I was coming back empty after delivering my load, because if I'd had a load, it would have taken way too much space to stop!"

Jack Barnes told us later that even though Kaylene had three times the distance to go that he did, she got to the child before he did and had picked her up and had run to the ditch on our side of the road and lay down with her. When Jack got to them, Kaylene was sobbing with relief. He tried to calm her and offered to carry the child back home, but Kaylene would not let go of her little sister until she put her down on our own porch steps. Both the driver and Jack told us that their greatest fear was that a loaded truck would come along from the other direction before anyone could get to our sweet baby! During the day, it was usual for many, many trucks to pass our house.

99

Dee's Support and Her Heartbreak

Another supportive thing for me, other than my strong husband, his love for his family, and his firm desire to make a good living for us, was having my sister Dee and her family living close by. She lived up the road about one-quarter of a mile from us and would often walk down, carrying her baby, Barbara, while walking beside her was her little boy, David. He was about the age of my Margene or a little younger, I believe. Dee was always there for me when I needed her. For instance, when Renee was having so much colic, Dee would come and sit just to hold her while I took care of the baby.

Dee really worried about Renee, saying once to me, "Rachel Periwinkle [I hated my middle name!], I'm afraid you won't be able to raise her," when Renee, who seemed prone to health problems, was having teething issues and severe congestion.

Then, the summer before Eileen was born when I was having problems with my pregnancy, Dee was there for me. And at about the same time, Margene started having a severe stuffed-up nose that at first we thought might have been an allergy problem. (Brad had suffered with an allergy, one he referred to as hay fever.) Dee was the one who noticed a bad smell about Margene's face and that the sinus area of her nose looked rather swollen. We got her in to see the doctor right away, and upon examining her, he asked if she could have gotten into any type of seed, such as beans or corn. As a matter of fact, earlier in the week, I had found her putting beans in her mouth when we were shelling beans to save for seed. Apparently, she had earlier been putting them in her nose!

Dee and I spent a lot of time together in late summer and fall, and our families became very close. Her husband, Barney, owned and worked in a mine and would stop in at our house to pick up the family, for he expected them to be there. When he came home, he would be solid black from head to toe, except around the eyes where he had worn protective goggles, from the coal dust that had settled upon him in his underground mines.

Sometimes Dee and I had gotten dinner together, and I would suggest to him, "Barney, why don't you go home and wash up so we can all eat together? Dee and I have cooked plenty for all of us so that our two families *could* share a meal together."

He would go home and wash up and return to eat with us. We always liked having meals together, and Dee liked to come to our house where there were kids with whom David could play. Barbara was just a baby, too little to be much company to him.

A sad, sad tragedy happened to Dee and Barney's family. David became suddenly ill and died within twenty-four hours. The doctor diagnosed it as meningitis. The illness came on so suddenly that Brad and I did not even know about it until the child was gone. Eileen was only a few days old, I seem to remember, when Barney came to our house in the early morning, the morning after David died, and gave us the sad news. I had had a very difficult delivery and so many postpregnancy problems that I really was not able to be there for her. I did go to David's funeral, but the doctor warned me not to stand on my feet while there. During the graveside services, I remember sitting in a kitchen chair Brad had brought from home. One thing that sticks in my mind about the wake and funeral was little Barbara, David's baby sister, worrying about her big brother in his coffin with socks on but no shoes! This tragedy was such a sad thing for my sister and her little family.

100

Beginning of Frightening Times

In mid-November, when Eileen was about two months old, I walked over to my husband's welding shop. I habitually kept my eye on his shop from the house, as several of our windows faced that direction. I knew when I saw constant flare from his welder that he was busy; however, it had been close to an hour since I had seen the last flash, and even though it was a little early for his lunch, I took it over to him. Once again, I found him sitting in the corner with what looked like a number of invoices spread around him, and he was jotting figures on a tiny pad before him. I walked over to the makeshift desk, and when he realized I was there, he began gathering up the invoices and stuffing them in a manila envelope. Again, I had seen the very worried frown on his face that I suspected was more than a frown of concentration. I asked him what was going on.

He paused only briefly and then said, "You may as well know." He picked up the manila envelope and started pulling out what he had just stuffed into it.

"These are invoices for jobs I've done for the mining company that are long overdue and that I doubt will ever be paid. I have hundreds of dollars' worth of work for which they owe me in addition to these. See all this work that they keep bringing me?" He indicated several large pieces of equipment in his shop. "I just told them this morning to come pick them up, for I won't do any more work until I'm paid for jobs I've already done. I think trying to get my money is useless. I expect them to go out of business at any time or at least to go bankrupt.

"I have to figure out something soon that I can do right away; I will very soon be out of coal to sell. I'll see if I can get some of the money owed me by having them pay me in coal, though I don't want to get in more coal than I can sell, as most people around here already have in their winter coal. I may have to haul it farther and sell to businesses in other places some distance away—maybe as far away as Louisville, Lexington, or Knoxville. To be honest, I think it'll be only days before Custer [owner of Osway Mining Company] closes all the strip mines around here. All the privately owned mines, anyway, are in the same mess."

Of course, as was usually the case with me when I heard news of serious problems to come, I became slightly panic stricken. "What will we do?" I exclaimed.

And as usual when I became scared, he immediately calmly reassured me. "I don't want you to worry, for I think I just about have it figured out. I will take care of it."

He always had taken care of any problem, and I knew he would this time.

101

Saved by the Railroad

By Thanksgiving 1952, it was obvious to all of eastern Kentucky that if the private-owned mines could stay open, it would be a miracle. On the Monday before Thanksgiving, with all his stockpiled coal sold, Brad decided to again look for the possibility of work in the Cincinnati area. He had to make a quick decision, as no jobs seemed to be available in our area, and our reserve cash was running low. As we had discussed long into the night, he had little choice but to go to Ohio to seek work. He left early the next morning, the Tuesday before Thanksgiving, for Cincinnati. Midday the next day, Wednesday, he called to the telephone of a business owner friend of his and left a message for me at his grocery store. The message conveyed that Brad had a job on the railroad—the same job he had left just after we were married —but they wanted him to start on the Monday after Thanksgiving. He said he had found himself a sleeping room and that he would be home early on Thanksgiving to take care of the loose ends at home. He said he didn't want me to worry, for he had more good news that he would tell me when he got home.

He had urged his friend to assure me that we were going to be all right. This was the first of many times my wonderful, caring husband was to say these very words to me, and we always were. He personally (with God to lead him) saw to it!

Brad got home after midnight on Wednesday. On Thanksgiving morning, when the children awakened and saw their dad home, their joy was something to behold! He had never been away from us before. They all piled on the bed, and I thought they might smother him. I brought the baby into the bed, and she kept grabbing his nose and giggling. The kids were no happier than their mom or dad, for that matter! As it was nothing unusual when it concerned his family, I saw him furtively wipe away tears of joy several times during the kids' welcome.

102

Crucial Plans in the Making

Brad and I had not had the opportunity to talk about the state of things in our life until after breakfast when I had the kids all settled with their games and the baby in bed for a nap.

Then Brad said, "How do you feel about moving back to Cincinnati?"

I was dumfounded for a moment and then answered, "If that's what we need to do, we'll do it."

He said, "Yes, I think it is. The long evenings when I was there alone and had nothing else to do, I did some serious thinking. I don't feel like my going there and taking a temporary job is the answer, for what new is going to happen to make it possible for me to be able to come back and find any kind of work to take care of our family like I want to? It's getting harder and harder to make a living in this area of Kentucky, and even though I was doing pretty well, I had to work all the time and spent very little time with my family. What I'm doing now takes me away from the family even more, and I don't want to be away. I'm also tired of working for myself with all the worries of taking care of everything that goes on with keeping my own business running. I want to be able to work my shift and leave the plant and worries behind when my shift ends. I don't mind working overtime a little— or a lot, for that matter; I just want someone else to have the worries of running that business."

He was sitting down and baring his soul to me. As he talked, I realized what a load that had been on him, and with his not wanting to worry me, he didn't talk to me about it until that moment. He felt he needed to protect me and, by doing so, had loaded himself too heavily. Granted, I had a lot going on, but with my recurring pregnancies and the care the family required of me, I had blithely gone on without noticing he needed help. I could look forward to the lightening of my load with no more pregnancies to worry about. It was then that I promised myself I would be more involved in what his family responsibilities were and step in where I could.

Brad had much more to talk about, and his news kept coming. In his time to stop and think, something else had come to mind. The oldest of our kids was Kaylene, who was twelve years old, and in just a few years, she would be in high school. Before we could turn around, she would be going on to higher education or looking for work, and Brad Jr. was not far behind her. The better economy brought to our part of Kentucky by the strip mining would fade with the companies leaving. He told me all this and more, and it had made him think, for the kids' sake, we had better move them to an area where employment opportunities would be there when the time came for them. He also told me his railroad job was just to be a stopgap measure until he could do better. He had leveled with the railroad, and they hired him anyway. But if I agreed to move to Cincinnati, we would tie up all the loose ends in Kentucky and move as soon as we could.

There was more! He had done a lot of thinking and planning while he was in Cincinnati. I was also to learn that he, as always, had very carefully thought things out before decisions were made. He would tell me what he thought we should do, and while often I was so scared we'd make the wrong decision, I hesitated to give my immediate approval, but he would eventually convince me. Never did he lead us astray; he seemed to always have the right intuitions. It helped to pray a lot, and I know he did!

He said that after examining the employment opportunities in Cincinnati, he had made application at General Electric, and the interview was very positive. He was told that they needed welders with his qualifications and experience; however, since they were near the end of their contract year, they were waiting until the new union contract before taking on new welders. He had learned that the department where welders were to be employed would be a newly classified job under the new contract. GE would be hiring in about six weeks. His hire status classification was to be "tentative hire," depending on results of his physical, which would not be done until after the beginning of the year. Knowing that it would be impossible for a man with a family to be unemployed with no income, some of the men placed in this tentative-hire category would not return, as they would need to find jobs sooner and would seek elsewhere. If hired, they would probably stay with the job. The tentative-hire status would give them that option. This would be what Brad would like to do if I agreed to go back to Ohio.

There was still more! While he was interviewing at General Electric, he was given a pamphlet listing possible dwelling opportunities for GE employees needing to relocate. He looked at the possibility of buying a house and saw some listed on the Kentucky side of the Ohio River in Covington. He found houses he thought might meet our needs and in a price range he felt we could afford.

One was a brownstone on a small lot. He looked at it and found it had been remodeled and repainted, and he thought I would like it. It would fit our family, with our girls sharing a large dormitory-like room on the second floor. It had a formal dining room that could be later converted to a bedroom for the older girls. It had a large eat-in kitchen with a ten-foot-long dining table and ten chairs that were to be left in the house. (The house had been used as a boardinghouse for workingmen away from home.) It turned out that Brad had placed a cash offer with the Realtor, who assured him his offer would most likely be accepted, but that since the owner was away for a family Thanksgiving, he couldn't confirm the owners' acceptance until the Monday following the holiday. That, too, needed my approval. He had certainly been busy!

The more we talked, the more excited I got, and the more I admired this good man (if that were possible ... I already believed he hung the moon!). His enthusiasm was catching. We prayed together to give our thanks on this Thanksgiving Day for all God had done to bring this big, loving family together and making them fit so well; we thanked the Lord for providing for us as He had and, more than anything, for bringing us together and blessing our love for each other. We asked God to help us make the right choices on the decisions we faced, for we were placing them in His hands.

We had lots of news to tell Brad's parents and his brothers and sisters when we later gathered at their house for a Thanksgiving dinner. Lots of his extended family members were there for the gathering that day, and we got to see many I had never met. So much good food and fellowship!

It was a wonderful gathering, and after other guests had gone, we told Ma and Pa of our plans. They were excited for us and offered to help in any way they could. They asked if we needed money, which Brad refused. He told them he had a little put away, enough to buy the house and make the move, and that he intended to try, in the next couple of days, to sell out and arrange to rent out our house, which should bring enough to give us a start in the new place. In the meantime, he explained, he did have a job—low paying, however, but one he could keep until he could get on at GE. With their best wishes, we got ready to leave, but not before making arrangements for Nolan (Brad's younger brother) to come up and watch our kids for an hour or so the next morning so that we could go into Denton to talk to my parents about our move. Ma and Pa had been so wonderful about it; I just hoped my parents would be as supportive, and I thought they would.

We arose from bed on the Friday after the holiday and, after breakfast, headed for Denton. We both felt we had God's blessings on the decisions we had made to go to Ohio. We told my parents about our plans, and they seemed thrilled for us too. Papa mentioned that a railroad coworker was looking for a dump truck to use for hauling gravel and might be interested in Brad's coal truck. Brad gave him the information about the truck and what he wanted for it, and Papa said he knew the man would get back to him. He did that very day and bought the truck. Mama was glad for us, but it was obvious she hated to see us go. Mama said she would help us in any way she could if we would just let her know what we needed. It seemed they were in our corner as well.

We broke the news to the children, and they seemed very positive about moving to a new, exciting place. Someone had told little Brad about Cincinnati's zoo, and that alone would have convinced him we should move. This seemed too much like an adventure for any of them not to be excited.

103

The Return

In the next two days, Brad accomplished miracles! He sold his truck and the tools and equipment in his shop and rented out our house, the tenants to move in as soon as we moved out. He turned his garage building over to his brother Daniel to use for a small business of his own. He ordered from a local coal dealer (a friend of his) and paid for a load of coal to be delivered to the house we were to buy. He was that certain we would get it. He contracted the same man (who had two trucks normally used for hauling coal) to move our household goods and furnishings to Covington, Kentucky.

It was so hard to spend the next eight weeks without Brad. He was able to spend a few days with us at Christmas and came home with presents for the kids and me. He had told me he would do the shopping for me since it would be hard for me to get away without him there to help. I sent him a list of possible things to get, and he did well, much to my surprise, for he had always left that kind of thing to me. He got me a beautiful gold-and-pearl necklace. I loved it! He told me his landlady (Liz, the same landlady he and I had when we lived in Cincinnati before and after we first got married) had wrapped the gifts for him, and she had written me a nice note.

It was wonderful to hear from our former landlady. She was so good to both of us when I was ill back in 1947. I saw her one time after we moved to northern Kentucky, and that was a few months after we moved to Covington, when she came to bring us a housewarming gift. She may have moved out of the area, for we never saw her again. She had told us she was selling her apartment building, for it was getting to be too much for her to manage. I don't know how old she was, but I would guess her to be older than our parents, somewhere in her mid- to late sixties.

On our move to Covington, we brought along our household furniture and appliances, cured hams, pork shoulders, and bacon, along with all our home-canned fruits and vegetables. We had sacks of flour, pinto beans, and potatoes. We were in good shape to be able to prepare a decent meal quickly, for all packages and boxes of foodstuffs were well labeled and together, making an emergency meal possible and in short order.

Our move was planned for January 24–25, 1953. Brad was to drive home after work on Friday, January 23, and with Daniel and his younger brother Nolan to help pack up and load the trucks on the twenty-fourth, we could then plan our move for early morning on Sunday the twenty-fifth. All things worked as planned, and we arrived at about noon on January 25.

Daniel drove one truck, and the owner of both trucks drove the other. Both men helped unload and set up our furniture. Kaylene was twelve, soon to be thirteen at the time, and was lots of help to me, so she and I took care of putting things in order in the bedrooms and kitchen while cooking the meal to feed the workers before they started back to Sunfish. Our coal had been delivered the week before, and everything was good, for the weather was cold! Brad was to be back to work on Monday morning, but not to the railroad. He had found a job at a small hand-truck manufacturing company, which paid more than the railroad and had hired him even after knowing his tentative-hire status at GE. This company was to come to the employment rescue for Brad yet another time in the near future.

104

Truly Blessed

We had come a long way, Brad and I, from love at first sight (speaking for myself, and Brad agrees that it was for him as well) at South Denton Missionary Baptist Church in Denton, Kentucky, to our being together at our present home on Pleasant Street in Covington, Kentucky, as a happily married couple with seven children! On that day in January 1953 as we prepared for bed our first night in our new home, we gathered all the kids together and stood in our new, almost empty living room. We looked fondly at this wonderful little gathering in our new home, barely holding back tears and trying to speak around the lump in our throats. Surrounded by the ones we loved most in the world, we thanked God for seeing us through times that had been rough but most rewarding because of the love we had for each other and for the promise our lives seemed to hold. We pledged to our blessed heavenly Father and to each other to lead our children in the way they should go; to do the best we could to make a good life for them; and to always keep God's teachings familiar to them by taking them to church. We pledged to provide for our children in their physical needs yet work to instill traits in them that would make it possible for them to be independent of us and as adults to be able to provide for themselves, while always loving them and each other with all our hearts.

We had overcome many hurdles facing us from day one, but as we had cleared each of them, we had become stronger and even more ready to tackle any to come. The Carrington family *was all right!*

Epilogue

The story of my life and the lives of my loved ones had only just begun. It became increasingly obvious as our lives progressed that my beloved Brad could manage money well from his hard-earned paychecks while supplementing that amount by his farm income. Never did he use the money for his personal leisure—any activities he organized always involved his family.

My life following our move to Ohio began to take on a multifaceted, chameleon-like appearance. Because we could afford time for leisure activities, as well as time to dream, my husband's active imagination came up with ideas that started our family down new roads—roads that were to lead to exciting places and activities!

Watch for the next segment, *Dreams Born; Dreams Fulfilled.*

CPSIA information can be obtained
at www.ICGtesting.com
Printed in the USA
BVHW070848111122
651211BV00002B/14